TEACHING DIFFICULT STUDENTS

Blue Jays in the Classroom

Nicole M. Gnezda

Rowman & Littlefield Education

Lanham • New York • Toronto • Oxford

2005

This title was originally published by ScarecrowEducation. First Rowman & Littlefield Education edition 2006.

Published in the United States of America
by Rowman & Littlefield Education
A Division of Rowman & Littlefield Publishers, Inc.
A wholly owned subsidiary of The Rowman & Littlefield Publishing Group, Inc.
4501 Forbes Boulevard, Suite 200, Lanham, Maryland 20706
www.rowmaneducation.com

PO Box 317
Oxford
OX2 9RU, UK

British Library Cataloguing in Publication Information Available

Library of Congress Cataloging-in-Publication Data

Gnezda, Nicole M., 1952–
  Teaching difficult students : blue jays in the classroom / Nicole M. Gnezda.
    p. cm.
  Includes bibliographical references (p.   ).
  ISBN 1-57886-175-6 (pbk. : alk. paper)
  1. Problem children—Education. 2. Behavior modification. 3. School discipline. I. Title.
LC4801.G64 2005
371.93—dc22

                                                                2005012708

⊗™ The paper used in this publication meets the minimum requirements of American National Standard for Information Sciences—Permanence of Paper for Printed Library Materials, ANSI/NISO Z39.48-1992.
Manufactured in the United States of America.

Dedicated to

Yvonne, Tony, and Katharine
who give me magnificent opportunities
to love and be loved

John, who brings peace, comfort, and fun into my life

and

Gary, whose legacy is still expanding

The woods would be very silent
if no birds sang except those that sang best.

—Henry Van Dyke
(Cited in Wilson, 1997, p. 18)

CONTENTS

List of Illustrations   vii

Acknowledgments   ix

Introduction: Blue Jays   xi

1   How the Universe Works   1

2   Vision   5

3   Why Kids Behave the Way They Do and
        What We Can Do about It   11

4   It Matters How We Treat Difficult Kids   51

5   It's All about the Soil: A Parable   55

6   Reconsidering Assumptions: Cleaning Out Our Brains   57

7   The Poor Get Poorer: Why Rewards and Punishments
        Do Not Work   79

8   We Won't Be Wimps!   85

9   More about Courage   97

10 Keeping It Simple   101

11 Why Bother?   105

12 The Ultimate View   113

References   119
Index   123
About the Author   127

ILLUSTRATIONS

Intro.1	*Blue Jay* by Nicole Gnezda	x
1.1	*The Universe* by Nicole Gnezda	xiv
2.1	*Pencil drawing* by Angela Quitar, student	4
3.1	*Untitled drawing* by Hallie Miller, student	10
3.2	*Self-Protection* by Kara Sherman, student	18
3.3	*Untitled drawing* by Clark Buchanan, student	21
3.4	*Untitled drawing* by Erik Bosko, student	40
4.1	*M.S. in October II* by Nicole Gnezda	50
5.1	*Cosmos* by Nicole Gnezda	54
6.1	*Untitled sculpture* by Callie Herman, student	56
6.2	*Competition* by Nicole Gnezda	62
7.1	*The Rich Get Richer and the Poor Get Poorer* by Nicole Gnezda	78
8.1	*Pencil drawing* by Sherman Hall, student	84
9.1	*Coeurage* by Nicole Gnezda	96
10.1	*Pencil drawing* by G. Anthony Smith, age 3	100
11.1	*Overworked* by Nicole Gnezda	104
11.2	*Self-Portrait* by anonymous student artist	106
11.3	*Letter* by anonymous student	111
12.1	*Gary's Signs* by anonymous photographer	112

ACKNOWLEDGMENTS

I have been blessed with friends, family, colleagues, and students who have helped me learn to live a better life. I wish to acknowledge my dear friends and confidantes, Amy Clark, herself an excellent and compassionate teacher, and Michelle Thomas. They listened to, supported, and elaborated on the ideas that became this book.

I wish to thank the following colleagues who have helped me process my teaching experiences and offered me great insights: Julia Woodrow, the late Pat Hamilton, Ron Porta, Lee Whitaker, Dr. Jeanne Orr, the late Jarvis Stewart, and Dr. Ray Swassing.

Special recognition goes to the family who raised me: my parents who taught me to love, Terry who taught me about children, and Eric who showed me it is possible to live your dream.

Most of all I want to thank all my students—the songbirds and the blue jays. I am honored that you trusted me enough to share yourselves with me, both through your words and artwork. Knowing you has made my life meaningful and taught me immeasurable things about the mystery of being human.

And of course I give my appreciation to Cindy Tursman, Marjorie Johnson, and Andrew Yoder, my editors at Rowman & Littlefield, for believing in my work and helping me through the publication process.

Intro.1. Blue Jay *by Nicole Gnezda*

Introduction

BLUE JAYS

During the monotonous gray of Ohio winters, birds are flashes of color. Even in the lushness of summer (and year-round in warmer climates), birds are beloved focal points in our yards. We set out food to attract them—thistle seed for finches, suet for woodpeckers, and sunflower seed for songbirds. We marvel at the miracle of their tiny bodies, their songs, and their flight. Our culture ennobles birds as signifiers of freedom, peace, and love.

Then there are blue jays. They cackle and screech. They pester other birds and scare them off the feeders. They are aggressive and nasty. Most of us want to shoo them away and we hope they never come back. But nature values these large, blue-hued yard birds that perch and give us time to see their brilliant colors. Blue jays are water-blue with white speckles on their wings, much like a reflective lake with waves spilling in the distance. Yes, there is, after all, beauty in the annoying blue jay.

In our classrooms, we have blue jays, too. They are disruptive and irritating. They won't follow directions, they act like they don't care, they pester or attack other children, and they argue with us. On days when they are absent, we secretly sigh with relief. They are not fun birds to have around.

But, like blue jays, our most difficult students have beauty to be found and we need to set our minds to finding it. We need to slow our heart-beats and feel our capacity to love. We need to look in these children's hidden places to find the secrets that will let out their beauty. Most important of all, we need to believe the beauty is there to be found.

Four-leaf clovers are hard to find, too, but I have collected hundreds of them. One day I found twelve at once, one for each month of the year. Yet some days I know I will not find any. After many searches, I learned the secret to finding four-leaf clovers: I have to believe they are there to be found. Believing effects how well I concentrate, how persistent I am, and how carefully I use my vision. Looking for beauty in our difficult students will require us to believe in them, too. We will have to concentrate really hard on our relationships with these students. We will have to be persistent in our dedication to find positive ways to connect with them. We will have to develop new ways to look at our students—to envision their realities, and imagine their possibilities. We will have to learn to see the bright blue on our blue jays.

The purpose of this book is to help as we teachers try to search out and actualize the beauty in each one of our students. It offers insights into the factors underlying our students' problem behaviors; support and inspiration in the midst of difficult relationships with young people; and a way to believe in our students' possibilities instead of their problems. It does not provide easy fixes, gimmicky management strategies, time-savers, or one-size-fits-all solutions. Instead, it offers *truths worth laboring for* (Spitzmueller and James, 2002, p. 49) and a plea to be concerned more with our students' internal selves than we are with mere control of our external classroom environments.

At first, the ideas presented in this book may seem simple, even trite. You have heard them before. We have all studied Maslow, Piaget, Erikson, and Glasser. But do we remember their theories? Do we implement them daily in our classrooms? Do we really understand the magnificence of their ideas and ideals? When this book asks us to ponder concepts of knowledge, empowerment, and love, our response may be, "been there done that." After all, the issue of knowledge has been around since that episode in Eden, empowerment is a common utterance on afternoon talk shows, and love is the number-one seller at Hallmark. But what this book really encourages us to do is to think anew about these concepts, this time with sensitivity to how they play out in our students' behavior and our own reactions to it. It invites us to look at our teaching from an ethical perspective that values the development of individual human beings more than the curricula we write, the facts we teach, and the grades we assign. It challenges us to become more compassionate caregivers of those young people who are invisibly afflicted with social ills not necessarily of their own making—our blue jay students.

Attending to our blue jay students with cognizance of and compassion for their underlying needs will require much of us. It will require us to examine our foundational beliefs; to think critically about our own behaviors; to overcome the inertia that keeps us set in our ways; to have the courage to change; and to accept the new approach as a long-term plan, not just a few "fits and starts" that will be doomed by lack of commitment and faith. It may take us into uncomfortable places, such as the political arena when we feel we must advocate for educational reform, or the depths of our own psyches when we connect with the essential humanness of all people—our students and ourselves. Most of all, embracing the new/old ideas in this book will ask of us that we make conscious choices for each day, each class, and each child about how we want to carry out our sacred responsibilities as teachers and developers of the future of our society.

Building successful relationships with our blue jay students is vital to the lives of these most needy young people and will affect their future roles in society. But it is vital to us, too. Loving them will humanize us and be very gratifying. It will reenforce our own feelings of value and competence. It will make it worth getting up in the morning and let us sleep peacefully at night. It is how we will make a difference in the world.

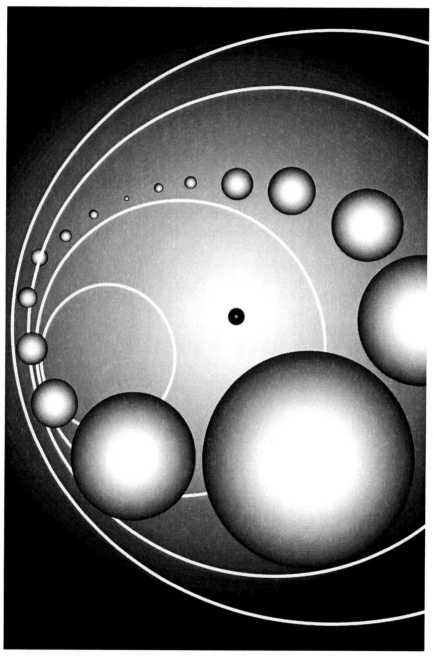

1.1. The Universe *by Nicole Gnezda*

●

HOW THE UNIVERSE WORKS

On the slopes of Mesa Verde in southwestern Colorado, I was awestruck by the contrasts I witnessed in the remains of a forest fire. There were yucca plants—blackened, gnarled, still as sculptures, and seemingly dead as can be. But from out of the roots, newly green stems reached hopefully toward the sky. Back home in Ohio, a walk in the deciduous woods presented similar contrasts. The lush foliage glimmered and swayed as it arched over my head, and the rich, nourishing scent of the woods sated my senses. The aroma, however, was not of flower nectar or sweet fruit, it was the smell of dead leaves, decomposing beneath my feet, cell by cell returning to the earth.

I have come to understand the universe as a balance of two primary forces—the force of entropy that erodes, collapses, and deconstructs life (Peck, 1978, pp. 263–268) and the force of creativity that adapts, redesigns, and gives birth to ever-new forms of living. Think about supernovas and red dwarfs, or how rotting fruit gives forth seeds for the future. According to many scientists, the universe is in an eternal process of contracting and expanding. Evidence of the balance of entropy and creativity is everywhere.

The forces of entropy and creativity are at work in our daily lives, as well. It has been stated ad nauseum that the only constant in contemporary life is change. Think about it. No matter how much we may want to stay still, to keep things just the way they are, no matter how difficult it is to adapt, we have only two choices: to grow or to get left behind to rot. A very alert and bright eighty-something-year-old former progressive and influential professor I know has been living in a nursing home for many years. The breadth of her life has shrunken to the size of her hospital bed table. Though still intellectually vibrant and personally charming, she can no longer create her artistic handmade holiday cards; and whenever we talk about computers she says with some sadness in her voice, "That world has passed me by." My professor is caught between the active creativity of her mind and the entropy at work on her body.

Every day we are all faced with opportunities to choose creative growth in order to balance out the entropy that is also busily doing its job in the universe and our lives. I believe that, as teachers, we have spoken loud and clear in favor of growth. That's why we teach. We get up way too early and begin a day that is way too full, have way too many conversations, do way too much paperwork, and hit the sack way too tired at way too late an hour. We do this for the most part because we believe in the importance of helping young people grow. We try to teach them to think in new ways, to spend their time on growth activities like reading, writing, making art and music, solving problems with numbers or experiments, and using their bodies to increase their physical potential. We choose creativity and growth! But we also see way too much entropy every day at school. One of the most difficult forms of entropy we have to deal with is that which has gotten hold of many of our students: the entropy that manifests as apathy, belligerence, giving up, violence, and failure. Students who exhibit these behaviors need our help to rediscover the joys of creative growth.

What can we do? Telling them over and over again what they are doing wrong, that they are behind, that they are lazy, that they are ruining their lives, or giving them punishments and low grades is not going to work. I know, because these strategies have not worked so far. By high school, students in trouble have been told these things since they were young and they are still in trouble. Pop psychologists often say that the definition of "crazy" is when someone knows that something doesn't work and stubbornly keeps on doing it anyway. Unfortunately, most schools continue to base their operations on a fundamental but flawed belief that many rules and increasingly severe punishments will force students to change their wayward behaviors. As a consequence, most school climates are dominated by disciplinary problems that are escalating in both frequency and magnitude.

In the following chapters, we discuss alternative ways to work with difficult students. These insights have come to me through twenty-five years of teaching and graduate study. They have been gleaned from what students have told me in our interactions and showed me in their artwork.

My hope is that by revitalizing our humanistic, creative forces and overcoming the forces of entropy in our teaching, we will enrich our classrooms and help our most difficult students to heal and choose creative growth for their own lives.

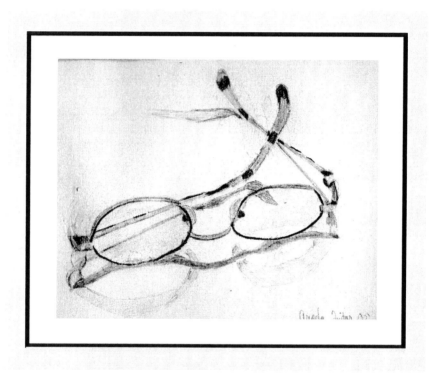

2.1. Pencil Drawing *by Angela Quitar, Student*

2

VISION

We think we see with our eyes. They are little sense organs that receive light rays and send them to our brains. Our eyes are sensitive only to light, not to things; therefore, what we see with our eyes are but tiny specks of light and areas absent of light. That's it.

How do we know that objects are in front of us, objects with identities, three-dimensions, colors, and that seem to have purposes and emotional significance? Our eyes are attached to neurons (brain cells) that take the patterns of light to the occipital lobes at the backs of our brains. From there, these patterns can travel to many other parts of our brains to be understood and conceptualized.

With repeated experience seeing objects, we develop brain paths, or "neural activity patterns" (Restak, 1984, p. 51) that we frequent. We often stereotype our responses to visual stimuli by following the same old brain paths, time after time, thereby missing other possibilities for interpreting what we think we are seeing. Optical illusions are an example.

The classic image of a lady's profile is seen by some people as that of a beautiful young lady and by others as that of a wrinkled up old lady. Once a person has made an interpretation of the image, it is often very difficult for him or her to see the alternative image that is also there, right before his or her eyes. Our brains jump to the easily accessible interpretation via the most commonly accessed brain path and sometimes get stuck there.

The destinations of our neural paths determine how we decipher and respond to what we have seen with our eyes. According to neuro-scientist, Richard Restak, "What we see is often dramatically different than what we have before our eyes" (p. 52). That is because our brains must decode the visual data (patterns of light) via systems for identification and interpretation. It is also because our previous experiences, knowledge, and emotions get involved in the process. Therefore, our understanding of what we see with our eyes is determined by what we are able and willing to see. In his book based on his PBS series, Ways of Seeing, John Berger stated, "We only see what we look at. To look is an act of choice" (1977, p.87).

Most often, being that we are a society that emphasizes left-brain style thinking and needs to label things to appreciate them, we first send these light images from our eyes to a place in our left cerebral hemisphere where they can be quickly identified and named. The quicker we can identify and name a visual sensation, the more at ease we feel, because we live in a society that likes decisiveness and quick closure.

We tend to identify these visual sensations according to previously learned categories. At a very early age, we are placed in front of objects and pictures of objects and taught their "names." My daughter Katharine's first phrase was "ut dat?" She would point at the things in our house and ask "Ut dat? Ut dat?" I would, then, enunciate the name of each object so that she might learn to say it, reenforcing in her the practice of labeling what she sees.

Though we are trained to name things, we are not as well trained to appreciate them or understand them. Think about how difficult it is for most people to enjoy abstract art, for instance. They are unable to appreciate the beauty of the rich colors of paint or the energy of the vigorous marks without knowing "what it's a picture of." Why? Because most people are trained, first and foremost, to identify the objects they are seeing, and since there are no nameable objects in highly abstract art, people get stuck and frustrated. In this society we have to be taught to enjoy visual sensations in their purer form, without letting our left-brain labeling system take over.

We also have to be taught that it is all right to delay closure, to live for a while without knowing what something is or what we are going to do about it. When we can put off labeling and closure, we can take time to experience the myriad possibilities for conceptualizing the things we see. We can begin to see subtle qualities, to understand the underlying reasons for things' existences, and to realize that everything we perceive visually and believe to be true is but a *cognitive interpretation* of simple sensory patterns of light waves.

Because the process of vision, seeing, and interpreting happens very fast, we believe that our eyes are doing all the work. In actuality, an imperceptible time-lapse occurs between the sensations of light in our eyes and the recognition of vision in our brains. Some scientists have hypothesized that this mini time lapse is the cause of the déjà vu experience. They suggest that sometimes we become slightly aware of our eye-vision and then, when our brains recognize what our eyes have seen, it feels as if we are living the moment for a second time—which, technically, we are. Vision, it turns out, is a quick but complex event involving our eyes, our occipital lobes, and a vast variety of neural pathways that can lead us to an infinite number of interpretations of what we see.

Now let us think about "vision" in its metaphorical state. Our "vision" is our view of the world: the things, people, and experiences in our lives. Like our eye-vision, it is a pattern of sensations that we interpret with our brains. As teachers, our vision—our interpretation of our perceptions—has major significance. Whether we see beauty or bad behavior in difficult students depends on our interpretations of what we observe. It is possible that our interpretations are "dramatically different" than what we have before our eyes?" (Restak, 1984, p. 51).

Classic interpretations of student behavior are easy to believe because they appear to have internal logic and our society has taught us to believe them. They seem correct because they fit the preestablished categories we have for decoding our observations. Classic interpretations of behavior are convenient, too. By quickly labeling a student, we free ourselves from having to think very much about how to understand and reach him or her. We can have a clear interpretation of and a quick closure to our problem.

Unfortunately, classic reactions to a blue jay student's behavior can be a rush to judgment. We fail to get to know the young person, to think, hypothesize, and test our interpretations of our observations. We also fail to identify and address the real roots of the inappropriate behaviors. We tell the student that "he has dug himself into a deep hole," or that she "has to start caring," or "just say no." Then we move on, leaving the student in as much pain, confusion, and ignorance as when he or she entered our lives. We have missed a great opportunity.

We have all observed disruptive, self-destructive, hurtful, and failure-oriented behaviors. We have also been taught by our professors and colleagues how to interpret these behaviors. When we see disengaged students, we interpret our observations as laziness. When we see argumentative students, we interpret them as "attitude problems." When we see substance abuse, we interpret it as a "bad choice." When we see angst and rebellion, we interpret them as "typical teenage behavior." But are we sure that what we think we are seeing is the correct interpretation of our observations?

I propose that, instead, we embrace the space between our eye-vision and our interpretations of that vision. That speck of time can be drawn out and employed. Once we observe a student's disturbing behavior we can delay our mental trip to the label center and begin our research. We can engage our student in conversation and do a lot of listening. We can compare her or his comments to knowledge we have about mental health problems, effects of abuse, and developmental psychology. And we can *feel with* the student—the root meaning of compassion. When we begin to feel what the student is feeling, we may begin to understand the student's motivations and coping mechanisms. We can experience the destroyed self-esteem, the intense fear of failure, the armor against abuse, the desperation for love and recognition. We can create a déjà vu for ourselves: first by perceiving the outward behavior, then, later, by developing a considered interpretation of it.

Now we can identify the source of the student's actions, or at least make an educated hypothesis about it. The step from here to a growth-producing relationship with a student—even a difficult student—is small and the consequences exciting. Lives can change, the young person's and ours. After bonding with us, our student may become more cooperative and respectful. The student may also reengage in learning, because in our class the student knows we care about him or her as well as his or her performance. We can offer the student information about alternative ways to respond to and seek solutions to his or her underlying problems. Because the student knows we care, he or she may even take our advice and begin to grow toward mental health and school success.

For us teachers, joy comes from connecting with a troubled young person and being a part of his or her change. It feels like saving a life. One difficult student at a time, we can all be heroes. Then we will have changed our lives, too. It starts with changing our vision.

3.1. Untitled Drawing *by Hallie Miller, Student*

3

WHY KIDS BEHAVE THE WAY THEY DO AND WHAT WE CAN DO ABOUT IT

During a job interview in 1986, I asked the middle school principal who was later to hire me, "Why do you think kids misbehave?" I was hoping to get information about his philosophy of education, style of discipline, the way he treated young people, and what he expected from his teachers in terms of classroom management. I was shocked by his answer: "Because teenage boys think about sex every fifteen seconds." It was only after I worked in his school the next year that I found out he had been having an affair with the assistant principal who occupied the office next door to his. I now assume, of course, that he was the one who was thinking about sex every fifteen seconds.

Wanting a more useful response, I spent the rest of my career looking for answers. As a result, I have identified four essential needs that seem to underlie the behaviors of young people. They are not new. People have always had these needs. Unfortunately, these needs are forgotten way too often during the course of most days at most schools. Being aware of these essential needs is, perhaps, the secret to great teaching. It enables us to understand our students, to build a productive rapport with them, to approach them in ways they can hear us best, and to work against the entropy in their lives. The essential needs are: knowledge, self-protection, love, and empowerment (Maslow, 1968; Brendtro et al., 1998; Glasser, 1969).

With these needs in mind, we can react to our students' behaviors with appropriate problem-solving strategies. The common, behaviorist approach of standardized punishments with little regard for the underlying motivations for behavior tends to exacerbate students' problems, increase their resentment, and precipitate retaliation and/or withdrawal. According to education expert William Glasser, "Any method of teaching that ignores the needs of . . . students is bound to fail" (1990, p. 23). A needs-based, problem-solving approach, however, encourages real growth and positive character change in our students.

KNOWLEDGE

The road to hell is paved with good intentions. Few people intend to bring harm to others, destroy the environment, or fail miserably at what they attempt. Yet the world is in many ways a hurtful, messy place! One reason is that most people operate on too much instinct and not enough knowledge. Ignorance may be no excuse for breaking the law, but it certainly is inherent in many mistakes made by reasonable people who are trying to live good lives.

For example, it is well known that abused kids often grow up into abusing adults. They probably wish to be better parents than the ones they had. Yet with the best of intentions, they become abusive anyway. Why? It's what they know. And what they don't know. Recently, there was a story in the local news of a young father on trial for abusing his one-year-old after the toddler had soiled its pants. The father sat there in court crying with regret for what he had done. So much heartache could have been avoided, I thought, if he had only had more knowledge to bring with him to his parenting tasks. He needed to know about age-appropriate potty-training techniques and, most important of all, how to manage his own overwhelming feelings. We may simplify this situation and just call him a "bad apple," or a "screwed-up kid" who never should have gotten someone pregnant in the first place. But, he would at least have had a chance to improve his life and his baby's if he had been operating from a position of knowledge rather than one of ignorance.

Many of our students are also operating from positions of ignorance about themselves, how they learn, and how to live with other people in positive, growth-producing relationships (Glasser, 1969, p. 22). They need information about mental health, cognitive styles, etiquette, media literacy, systemic prejudice, and conflict resolution. Young people whose families have not provided them with this necessary life-information show up at school awkward, resistant, rude, volatile, aggressive, provocatively dressed, and behaving in offensive ways.

We adults are often appalled when we watch students interact with each other and with us. Though we assume they understand the rules of civil social interaction, our blue jay students often do not. Since they don't get it, they also don't get why we are so put-off by them. We slap punishments and more rules on them and become more frustrated when they do not obey the new rules any more than they obeyed the old ones. We hassle them and they hassle us back. We are at an impasse because we assume that our students possess our knowledge and, therefore, understand our perspectives about how to live.

Once during a staff meeting at my school, when we were—for the umpteenth time—complaining about students' dress and what consequences we should impose on them for showing their boxer shorts or their cleavage, I suggested that first we should educate them about the messages they were conveying with their clothes. Being an art teacher, I had learned about the history of fashion and had been struck by the clear relationship between clothing styles and the roles of women in society. I thought that a school assembly about fashion history and women's rights might prove very interesting and empower girls to make more informed choices about their clothes. Before I finished my first sentence, I was booed by my colleagues. End of story. The assembly was not proposed. The girls in my school still walk around dressed more like sex objects than scholars, and they don't even realize it. They have learned about dress and behavior from the popular media, but they haven't learned about them from reasonable adults like us.

Children are cognitively geared to learn about rules and expectations during their elementary school years, according to developmental psychologist Jean Piaget (Piaget and Inhelder, 1969). At this a time, kids realize there are specific ways that things operate. For instance, they thirstily learn about the rules of letters (phonics), of grammar (reading and writing), of numbers (arithmetic), of cursive writing, of games, and of etiquette (Mr., Mrs., please, thank you, wait your turn, raise your hand, etc.). They even learn the rules of play, how to share, and not to hurt others. Ever wonder why a young child will run to an adult to tattle on someone? It is not because the child is hatefully trying to get someone else in trouble. It is because he or she wants acknowledgment that a rule exists and was broken.

This is the stage when children should be learning how to function academically in school and socially in the world at large. It is also a time when they *want* to learn how to do this. Unfortunately, many of our blue jay students have missed this opportunity to learn the rules of life. "Normal" parenting and teaching styles that are big on punishments and scolding are often negligent in helping young people to understand the underlying structures of society, its institutions, and the impact of people's actions on those around them. Young people who are thirsty to understand (Glasser, 1992, pp. 44–45) are, instead, being trained to obey (or not) without a grounded understanding of why.

What Can We Do about Knowledge? Educate!

A fifth-grade boy taught me this. He had just transferred into the school at which I was teaching and on the second or third day at his new school he hit a boy with whom he was arguing. I went to him and, instead of raising my voice or taking away his recess, I took the time to explain alternative problem-solving strategies. He looked back at me with great big, dark eyes and said thoughtfully, "Oh. I wasn't raised that way. I'll try that next time." I believe I was seeing his mind stretch and his good heart open to new possibilities of social interaction. While he obviously did not make a complete one hundred eighty–degree change in his personality, he did begin to relate to life differently. He realized that there are ways to act other than the instinctual responses on which he normally relied. He learned to think about his behavior instead of seeing it as something "I can't help." That day, rather than being angry with him or punishing him for what he would not have understood to be wrong, I educated him. After all, to educate is our duty.

As much as we teachers express concern about "kids today," we are, unfortunately, not offering young people enough organized opportunities to learn needed life information. Learning how to live is not included in the curricula, the scopes and sequences, nor the standardized tests that drive the content of our classes. However, it could and should be. For instance:

- Life-skills classes that teach about child development, conflict resolution, and healthy family relationships are offered in many middle and high schools, but are usually electives that only a minority of students ever take. Schools could make these classes available, desirable, and/or required for the general school population. (Information available in Home Economics or Family and Consumer Science curricula.)
- Media literacy could be integrated into the teaching of computer skills, language arts, speech, and/or visual arts. Students could learn how to analyze visual information and defend themselves against the potent messages of pop-culture perpetuated by the media. (Information available in a variety of resources by the Center for Media Literacy, www.medialit.org.)
- We admonish students by telling them to go home and study, when we should be improving their achievement by teaching them study strategies specific to their own particular cognitive styles and personality types. (Recommended authors include Levine [2002]; Springer and Deutsch [1981]; Lawrence [1982]; Briggs-Myers [1990].)
- We assume that prejudice doesn't exist in our schools unless someone spray-paints a swastika or the "n-word" on a wall. Many schools only teach about prejudice occurring in past events—the Holocaust or the pre–Civil Rights South. We could organize seminars and activities to engage students in discussions about the reality of prejudice in their own environments, helping them to recognize the racism and sexism that are still prevalent in daily life. (Recommended resources include Teaching Tolerance, www.tolerance.org/teach; J. Banks [1994]; C. Gilligan [1982]; The American Association for University Women, www.aauw.org/research/index.cfm.)
- Many schools have peer-mediation programs that offer instruction in conflict resolution, and I applaud them. If most schools are like mine, however, many of the students who need most to learn mediation are the ones who resist and even make fun of the program. These students could be required to participate in peer mediation or other training in conflict management as a part of the school

disciplinary response to their behaviors. (Information and training available through M. Trichel and J. D. Davis at the Interfaith Center for Peace, http://peace-center.org.)

- Principals, deans, and other disciplinary officials could include anger-management strategies in their repertoire of responses to student misbehavior. (Contact the American Psychological Association, www.apa.org/pubinfo/anger.html.)
- Etiquette is a set of behavior expectations for civil interaction between people. Adults establish school rules and regulations in which standard etiquette is implicit but is news to many kids from dysfunctional families, diverse backgrounds, or age-groups different from the teachers. Why not offer kids an explanation of the underlying reasons for certain behaviors and for the restrictions against others? Let us teach them both the rules and values of standard etiquette.

Information about how to live successfully in a community could be provided to kids without much expense to a school system. It is a way of proactively educating young people, thereby avoiding many problems down the road.

What if a school does not or will not make these positive changes? All is not lost. Many wise people believe that change occurs not through new programs or political agendas but by affecting one person at a time. In our day-to-day interactions with our students we can easily slide in information about learning styles, facilitate discussions about coping with real-life events, recognize and discuss biases in school and the world at large, explain the reasons behind our rules, and teach conflict management as the need arises in the classroom. It is my experience that students are very appreciative whenever we connect with them as human beings and offer them help in navigating this very confusing world.

A third way to teach necessary life skills is by modeling them. We must take care to be fair and polite and to problem solve the differences we have with our students. We need to be very careful about how we interact with those whose ethnicity, race, or gender is different from our own. We need to be a daily example of sensitivity to individual needs. We need to follow our own conflict-management format when we interact with difficult kids. We also need to model mental health (that means take care of ourselves psychologically) and respect the mental health situations of our young people. Students are not only ill-equipped to recognize, deal with, and seek help for their emotional vulnerabilities, but are often misunderstood or further upset by teachers' reactions to them.

For instance, "Leslie" was a sixteen-year-old girl who came back to school after in-patient treatment for drugs and panic disorder and who, I later learned, had been a victim of repeated sexual abuse. She had Kool-Aid red hair, a sneer on her face, multiple piercings, and little energy. If she came to school at all, she spent time in the art room painting abstract expressions of her feelings, and when it was necessary for her to go to another class, she cried, trembled, and cowered in the doorway, afraid to go. In an emotional phone conversation, her distraught mother told me angrily of an incident that occurred in our school. According to protocol, a conference between Leslie's mother, her teachers, the guidance counselor, the school psychologist, and the assistant principal was held to discuss Leslie's precarious mental situation and the terms of her reentry to school. Soon after, the assistant principal confronted Leslie in the hall and, rather than supporting her struggling efforts to readjust to school, he threateningly accused her of faking her mental illness. I suppose that he believed he was being a strong disciplinarian, but in truth, his insensitive, punitive approach exacerbated the girl's already self-destructive school phobia. Leslie was brutalized once again by a powerful adult.

To be sensitive and effective teachers of life skills, we must first educate ourselves. We need to know about mood disorders, substance abuse, the long-term effects of child abuse, developmental psychology, the variety of learning styles, personality type theory, differentiated teaching methods, active listening, systemic racism, gender bias, sexual orientation issues, and conflict-resolution strategies. Only then can we approach our students with the authority to understand them; only then can we model appropriate behaviors for them; and only then can we guide them to live their lives in less entropic ways.

SELF-PROTECTION

"Nathan," nearly two hundred pounds and only eight years old, had his arm around the neck of a classmate—again. He seemed innately aggressive,

3.2. Self-Protection *by Kara Sherman, Student*

using his size to retaliate against any child who he thought was ridicul-
ing him. He strangled, hit, and sometimes sat on his classmates. Once
again, I put Nathan in time-out. Later, we had a heart-to-heart. I listened to his complaints about how the kids picked on him relentlessly. I offered sympathy, but also tried to broach the subject of his weight. I

thought he probably had some underlying issues and that he might want to seek help for them, thereby beginning to solve the problem of his overeating and eventually improve his social life. When I politely mentioned his size, he threw his arms across his chest and, with tears in his eyes, proclaimed, "I need my weight!" Nathan lived in a state of self-protection.

We all have layers of protection we have built around ourselves, though most are not as visible as layers of excess body mass. I call my layers "my cocoon." Earlier in my life, my cocoon was pretty thick. I had been living life the way I thought I was supposed to instead of how I needed to and was using many unconscious defense mechanisms to keep me going during difficult times. I built up so many layers of protective cocoon that I could hardly sense the true, creative self that was hidden away inside.

Let us each think for a minute about our own particular type of protective coating. Is it a domineering personality? Perfectionism? Inflexibility? A great whine? Overachievement? The unequaled ability to argue? A need for control? Withdrawal? Maybe even physical aggressiveness? In our youths, most of us were wounded by our parents, teachers, peers, and/or other circumstances—some of us very deeply. As a result, we all developed our own cocoons to protect the hurt and scared essential selves that we started out to be, once upon a time.

So it is with our students. Only those with humane family histories or years of counseling are able to function without thick cocoons surrounding them. Many show up for school with not just cocoons to protect them, but with personal armies on alert. Belligerence, aggression, and violence are their armies, ready to protect them from the anticipated next assault to their already wounded selves. The thing about our students' cocoons and armies is that they are usually invisible. What we teachers see, instead, are the bullying behaviors and oppositional attitudes that come from psyches deeply in need of protection.

For example, most students are experts at gauging what to wear to school and what language to speak in order to impress their peers and avoid being rejected socially. They already know that anything is better than social rejection. Their extreme styles of dress and profane language are the very currencies with which they purchase acceptance and protect themselves from ridicule.

Self-protective devices go much deeper than fashion and language, however, and have greater costs. For instance, do we ever ask ourselves why there is so much apathy among students these days? I don't believe in apathy. I think something else is going on, something that only looks like apathy: many students are really protecting themselves from the fear and pain of failure by pretending to be apathetic (Glasser, 1992). Trying to succeed must seem impossible and risky to these already suffering young people, so they convince themselves that they don't care. Experience has taught them that if they care about school, truly want to achieve, invest themselves in it, and then fail, the pain will be intolerable. For students whose school histories have been covered with red marks, poor grades (for some students that means Cs or even Bs), criticism from teachers, and files of disciplinary forms, failing one more time would be too emotionally risky—unless they control the failure.

To fail on purpose is a kind of success (Oremus, 2004). So is setting one's standards so very low that achieving them is practically guaranteed. This is often called "sliding by with a D," another manifestation of the defense mechanism apathy.

These days, one of the major symptoms of student self-protection, and so-called apathy, is school absence. Admit-slips excuse certain students for frequent illness; some parents say that their children are too tired to go to school or need a "mental health day." Students have an even wider variety of excuses, sometimes cutting class just to hang out with friends. However, students without major illness who miss school frequently do so for primarily one reason: School is not a nurturing place for them to be. They cannot continue to risk their secretly wounded and scared inner selves day after day, so they escape. The ultimate result of school apathy and escape is what Hoffman and Levak call "devastating drop-out rates" (2003, p. 30).

Some students with more serious self-protective needs exhibit symptoms of recognized psychological syndromes that also manifest as apathy. One is passive-aggression (American Psychiatric Association, 2000, pp. 789, 791). When a young person does not believe himself or herself to have the power to change a situation that is causing emotional pain or to get help for personal or family problems, he or she may become passive-aggressive and gain power by refusing. Refusing to involve himself

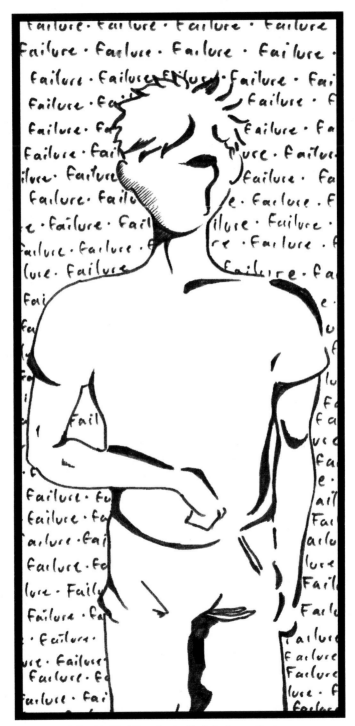

3.3. Untitled Drawing *by Clark Buchanan, Student*

or herself in school, refusing to value school, refusing to succeed at school, refusing to do homework, or chores, or follow family rules can be power-plays to get back at adults or call out for help. These acts of resistance feel to a young person like self-assertion and personal strength, though in an unconscious, unexamined way. Passive-aggressive resistance may be inaccurately interpreted by adults as apathy or defiance.

Other young people who have suffered psychological injuries may react by "numbing-out" or, in the extreme, dissociating from the discomfort of their lives (DSM-IV-TR, 2000, p. 532). They have learned long before they enter our classrooms how to disengage their interior selves from the outside world, to "disembody myself from the boy who was getting beaten," as author Pat Conroy put it in his autobiography *My Losing Season* (2002, p. 340). Our students may look us in the eyes and act as if they are hearing our admonitions and criticisms, but they psychically remove themselves from the scene. We teachers think that we are clearly and effectively communicating to our students, our students may even nod in apparent understanding, but their behaviors never change. So many times I have heard myself say, "Why don't these kids get it? They don't seem to care that the grading period was over and they didn't turn in their main project. They seem to be going through the motions with no reaction whatsoever to failing." What better way for an unempowered, wounded, and hopeless young person to escape the pain of his or her "losing season" than to simply not feel it?

By examining the underlying nature of apathy, we see that it is usually not a lack of caring, but an embedded reaction to having once cared and been repeatedly and deeply wounded by rejection, failure, and/or emotional abuse. Apathy, therefore, is a strategy for self-protection.

Some students with exaggerated needs for self-protection do not succumb to apathy, dissociation, or passive-aggression. They come to school and vigorously act out instead of copping out. They "talk back," "mouth-off," and confront us. They proclaim their battle cries: "School sucks," "I am never going to use algebra, anyway," and "The teacher is unfair." They often pick on weaker or culturally different students, as well (Glasser, 1992).

Why does this happen? Because the best defense is a good offense—self-protection, again. When students grab control of a conversation, blame us, threaten us, or reject us, it is the same as putting up their armor. They approach us with their toughest personality in front, passionately trying to divert or avenge any potential new strikes at their already wounded senses of self. Toughness feels like competence and righteousness. It protects them from a blow they fear might just destroy their spirits once and for all.

Of course, neither we nor our students see their self-protective acts of aggression or withdrawal as what they really are. We see bad behaviors, bad attitudes, and apathy. They see mean teachers and boring schoolwork. Underlying both interpretations of school problems, however, are blatant manifestations of self-protective cocoons at work.

What Can We Do about Self-Protection?
First, Do No Harm, Second, Foster Success

Trilliums are wildflowers indigenous to Ohio woodlands. They are either white or the deep red of fresh blood. Their name is derived from the fact that they have three identical petals arranged atop three slightly larger leaves. I learned about them in third grade and, though I have seen only two or three in my whole lifetime, I am still in awe of them. They are sedately beautiful, and what impresses me most is their fragility. If a blossom is plucked, the entire plant withers and dies off forever. I tread near a trillium with careful steps and kneel down to view its beauty with complete awareness of the potential I pose for devastation.

So it should be with our difficult students. Though they act like irritating blue jays on the outside, on the inside they may be as vulnerable as trilliums. We probably will never know which ones are tough and resilient and which ones are on the verge of devastation; which spirits will give up on their dreams and themselves, turn on others, or live the rest of their days, as Thoreau put it, "in quiet desperation" (Bode, 1975, p. 263). Therefore, we must tread carefully around our difficult students, always aware of the potential we pose for devastation. Maybe we cannot save a child from the pain and dysfunction in his or her life, but with kindness and sensitivity we can be sure not to pluck his or her final blossom. We can be cognizant of the warning "First, do no harm."

Our negative reactions to students have long-term effects. When my daughter Yvonne was in first grade she had an insensitive teacher who greatly misunderstood her. The teacher complained about Yvonne's immature behavior (though her behaviors were age-appropriate), would not let her read until her phonics pages were colored neatly in the lines (though she had been reading since she was three), and punished her frequently. Before long, my bright and inquisitive six-year-old quit trying to read and started copying answers off other kids' papers because she was afraid to make a mistake. It was December when I found out what was going on, and I immediately switched her to a class with a highly nurturing, supportive teacher. I thought the problem was solved.

However, Yvonne continued to have self-esteem issues in school, as evidenced five years later when I had her accompany me to a parent-teacher conference. This time, the teacher gave Yvonne rave reviews on her learning, behavior, and social development. Yet as we walked across the playground on our way home, Yvonne asked me with a perplexed expression on her face, "Mommy, how could my teacher say such nice things about me when I am such a bad student?" The negative effects of only four months of first grade with a demeaning teacher had left damage that lingered well into Yvonne's future. I was shocked and saddened. And from then on, I was especially careful of how I spoke to my own students.

The least we can do for our blue jay students is to not exacerbate their feelings of shame and worthlessness. Remember, students who are apathetic or acting out in school are most likely young people who have been beaten down by their earlier home and school experiences and who cover their hurts with bravado, aggression, and/or withdrawal. Instead of hitting them with more criticism and anger, we need to help them heal, grow, and regain a belief in their own potentials. We need to promote our students' self-worth by nurturing, educating, and problem solving instead of scrutinizing, blaming, and punishing them. Self-worth is a basic human need (Glasser, 1969, pp. 12, 14).

Sometimes we blame students in order to alleviate a sense of our own failure (Brendtro et al., 1998, p. 20). When students continue to misbehave in our classes, we salve our growing feelings of incompetence by telling ourselves that these kids have character flaws that make them unteachable. If a student regularly sleeps in class, for instance, we may tell ourselves that the child is apathetic and lazy and, thereby, protect ourselves from having to think we might be boring. Sometimes we blame and punish kids because it is an easier response than trying to figure out what to do to help them. In addition we have been programmed to use stereotypical terms such as "lazy," "unmotivated," or "hyper" as if they were valid diagnostic descriptors.

I am not suggesting that we not hold students accountable for their actions, but we need to be very careful that our actions as teachers serve to support, nourish, and educate our young people, not to encourage further entropy. The instinct to blame and punish may be substituted with a motivation to delve deeper into the underlying causes of the student's troublesome behaviors. Otherwise, if we allow ourselves to be satisfied with blaming and punishing a kid, we give ourselves permission to stop trying to reach her or him.

I realize that there are young people with mental health problems and family dysfunctions that are way beyond our potential to fix; we are teachers, not psychiatrists or social workers. However, I also believe that there are many student problems we can help ameliorate if we do not quit trying so easily.

Rather than punishing kids for problems that may need serious psychological attention, we can offer them guidance and helpful insights. When students misbehave, for instance, we usually scold them and assign them a "consequence" (punishment) such as missing recess or serving detention. Instead, a conference with the student or his or her parents about possible mental health issues and interventions may be more responsive to a student's underlying situation.

"Brad" is an example. He sat at the side of the room with other off-task students. He was progressing quite slowly on his project, vacillating between a blank stare and animated social conversation. At a conference, his parents talked about his at-home demeanor in descriptors that resembled the symptoms of depression. The teacher posed follow-up questions and then carefully asked if they had ever considered that Brad might be having trouble with depression. To the teacher's surprise, they responded, "He had been on an antidepressant, but he quit taking it a couple months ago . . . his brother is our real concern, he is bipolar." The teacher explained that it is common for people to go off their antidepressants and then relapse. She also suggested that if one member of a family has a mood disorder then it is likely that other members could have a tendency for one, too. She recommended a return visit to their son's doctor. The parents were appreciative of the information. Within a couple of weeks, Brad was a different young man. He seemed energized, had a keen sense of humor that had previously not surfaced, had completed his art project skillfully, and was moving forward on the next one. His teacher told him he seemed different. "Oh, I started taking my medication again," he announced with a grin. Dealing with the underlying problem and educating the parents turned out to be much more successful than punishing him with poor grades or Saturday school.

Another example is "Justin." A good-looking, popular, and athletic high school junior, he seemed to be a slacker in class. He was never argumentative nor disorderly, but spent more time socializing than accomplishing any real work. I did not see him as a young man with a problem but as a kid with a disrespectful attitude toward school. I responded to him with admonitions to get to work and with poor grades. Several weeks into the semester, his mother requested a conference with all of his teachers. In a poignant story punctuated with honest tears, she related the history of Justin's downward spiral into clinical depression and a suicide plan. I was shocked. I had sensed none of this. Looking back, I now realize how important it must have been for him to maintain the appearance of "cool" in front of his macho male and adoring female friends. His mother continued to explain that he believed his continual struggle with school and his failure to succeed had precipitated his depression.

The next day Justin was in my class, I casually said a few words to him about the conference and offered to help in any way that I could. Then I tried something I had not done before. I offered to meet with him to do a learning-styles assessment, just to see if we might find out why school learning was so difficult for him. He agreed. We met during my prep-period and I asked many questions. I pulled out a questionnaire I had developed in grad school that sought to identify markers for individual learning styles and personality types. We found out that Justin was primarily a "right-brain," visual and kinesthetic learner with additional characteristics that were not consistent with the lecture/

reading/note-taking/show-your-work style of most classrooms. We also developed a list of strategies to help him adapt his learning style to the requirements of his classes. Over time, Justin and I became quite fond of each other, and his classwork and demeanor seemed to improve. He never became a great artist, but at least was more motivated in his attempts at art making.

A year later he was in my late husband's English class and, believe it or not, his grades had improved to nearly all As. According to my husband, Justin attributed his improvement to the interactions he and I had had about his learning style. I am sure that the coexisting treatment for his depression was also a major factor in his success. Justin went on to college and for as long as I kept in touch, was earning excellent grades.

Unlike the problem-solving approaches used with Brad and Justin to address their underlying psychological and cognitive problems, the traditional reward-and-punishment approach tends to backfire. Glasser (1992) uses the term "coercion" in reference to teachers' use of criticism, punishment, and low grades to try to force students to do what the teachers want. Once coerced, according to Glasser, a student's "main agenda becomes resistance" (p. 29).

For instance, in response to the insult of a punitive or critical act by an adult, the student naturally feels anger and resentment. The consequences are threefold. The student, who now feels hurt (even if her or his own behavior precipitated the punishment), may wish to retaliate, fight (verbally or even physically) to prove herself or himself right, and/or withdraw emotionally from the situation. The first two responses result in protracted power-struggles between students and faculty, the third, in apathy or truancy.

Because these students are young, they are not aware of the reasons for their resentment, only that they have it. To further protect their already compromised senses of self-worth, they may refuse to examine their own behaviors for fear of finding fault with themselves; instead, they use the defense mechanisms of denial and projection to vindicate themselves by blaming the adults. It becomes a vicious cycle of blame and punishment from both teachers and students, with little potential for real student growth or personal change.

But don't we have to do something when students misbehave? Of course we do, but just doing "something" isn't enough. We need *to do something that promotes growth and strengthens a student's sense of his or her own worth.* We have to listen, be fair, problem solve, and teach. We have to recognize and affirm the dignity and value of *every* human being in our classrooms, even when we are dealing with disciplinary issues.

This is how. First, we should establish in our classes the expectation that all members are to be treated with respect for their self-worth. I tell my students that none of us has the right to take away another's importance by using demeaning words or actions. Second, during episodes of conflict with individual students, we can follow this sequence:

Step 1—Provide time for angry or frustrated students to vent, to disempower the energy of their emotions.

Step 2—Be sure to understand the story, both sides if two people are involved. Active listening, in which the adult restates what he or she heard the students say, verifies the information and communicates to the students that they have been heard.

Step 3—Help students to identify the root motivations (underlying feelings) for their misbehavior. Examples might be self-protection, fear of failure, lack of empowerment, and violation of rights or dignity.

Step 4—Teach them about the real-world consequences of their inappropriate behaviors. Does their teasing hurt someone's already shaky sense of self-worth? Does hitting another student precipitate even further violence and make them less likely to get their problem solved? Does their ethnic joke contribute to the hatred and violence in the world? Does their tardiness to class disrupt your sense of order? Do their continual absences cause them to miss important information and subsequently to fail classes?

Step 5—Suggest more functional ways for them to solve their problems, such as anger-management techniques and mediation strategies to improve their interactions with others, journaling and art-making to vent their feelings, or breathing and relaxation activities to calm them down. Send them away with a plan for new ways to react to triggering stimuli.

Step 6—Let them know that you will be available to them in the future if they need to talk more.

When we respond to inappropriate student behaviors in these ways, we teach self-discipline by helping students to make sense out of their seemingly chaotic lives and by providing them with more functional coping skills (Brendtro et al., 1998, p. 29). We empower students with increased self-understanding, then motivate them to grow positively (Kohn, 1993, p. 59). We imbue students with feelings of self-worth because we show these young people that their actions really do affect the world and that we care enough to spend time with them working things out.

We avoid entropy because we do not contribute to the downward spiral of blame, punishment, denial, projection, and hurting back. When our students act in entropic ways, we need to react in creative, growth-producing ways. As a result, we will be character builders and help keep the universe in balance.

Another important duty for teachers is to promote students' emotional growth is to foster their academic success. Psychologists know that success creates feelings of competence, which not only contribute to a person's mental well being but also motivate him or her to continue attempting new tasks. This is called "competence motivation" (White, 1959). Just as school failure breeds self-protective apathy, success at learning breeds the desire to learn more. It is not hard to understand that we all choose to do those things that we know we can do easily and well and try to avoid doing things that are frustrating and at which we expect to fail. It is common sense. In college, for instance, how many of us took nuclear physics, advanced statistics, or figure painting just for the fun of it? Didn't we choose our majors because they were the subjects we were good at and those about which we loved to learn?

Our blue jay students, however, have few school subjects they love because they have not been empowered to succeed at learning. They may have atypical cognitive styles, require one-on-one instruction, or process only small doses of information at a time. Most likely they learn in ways that are very different from the way most of us teach.

"Differentiated teaching" is a catchphrase these days. What it means is that we need to teach to each of our student's unique configurations of cognitive strengths and weaknesses. Let's consider for a minute the infinite range of possibilities.

- Information enters the brain via three basic routes—visual (eyes), auditory (ears), and kinesthetic (active use of the body and all the senses). Each individual person has his or her own particular combination of strong and weak routes through which to receive information.
- There are myriad modes of processing information that can occur. Included are imaging, patterning, speaking words, reading words, global understanding, focusing on detail, integrating knowledge, sequencing information, multidirectional thinking, metaphorical thinking, memorization, critical thinking, and creative thinking, just to name a few.
- A variety of methods of information output can help students demonstrate what they have learned. Oral and written reports, private conferences, computer simulations, dramatic performances, real-life experience, and hands-on presentations are some possibilities. Oh yes, and there is also the written test.

  Though the test is the most common and highly touted instrument for assessment, it is only adequate in assessing certain kinds of information and for only certain kinds of students. Students with nonmainstream cognitive styles or cultural backgrounds may be at a disadvantage just because they are asked to show their learning in a test format.
- Common, identifiable learning weaknesses include dyslexia, other language deciphering disabilities, auditory discrimination problems, short-term and long-term memory weaknesses, dysgraphia, speech disorders, distractibility, attention span difficulties, and many more.

Because there are as many combinations of preferred styles of input, processing, and output of information as there are variations of cognitive weaknesses, the total number of cognitive strength/weakness permutations is enormous. Even if we limit our statistical speculation to the twenty-five or thirty students in one of our classes, we can still imagine the wide range of learning needs we teachers face each day.[1]

An understanding of differentiated learning styles requires us to reconsider the limitations of the methods of teaching we have grown up with and been trained to use. It asks us to get to know the learning potentials of our blue jay students and adapt our teaching to meet their untapped abilities. We have to use a variety of methods to teach the variety of students that we have and change the pace of our teaching to parallel the pacing of our difficult students. One way to do so is to build into our schedules time to work one-on-one with our students. Another is to assign to each student only the quantity of work he or she is able to handle. A third way is to assess (not necessarily grade) the stages of the learning process as well as the final outcomes. A fourth is to evaluate our students' effort, engagement, and overcoming of obstacles. A fifth way is to set short-term goals for those who need them, verbally reward them every fifteen minutes for staying on task, or briefly check their papers after each page of a draft is written, for instance.

To adapt our teaching to the range of learning needs in our classrooms may seem like a great deal of work—more work than is humanly possible. I understand. But I have learned through experience that by implementing individualized approaches to teaching and assessing students, I have also avoided much of the hard work and heartache of power-struggles and disciplinary actions with difficult students. The rewards of differentiated teaching, multiple formats for assessing, positive reenforcement of small successes, and the subsequent reduction in behavioral disturbances are compensation for the initial effort it takes to revamp and individualize our teaching. For the sakes of our blue jay students and our own nerves, we need to consider expanding our teaching repertoires so that we can more effectively reach all our young learners, help them to begin finding success in learning, and acknowledge their successes repeatedly each day.

Eventually our students, even our blue jay students, will begin to see their academic potentials. They will begin to feel competent and subsequently become motivated to engage in further academic pursuits. Not all students will want to study nuclear physics, statistics, or advanced art, but they will all have the chance to develop a positive, rewarding experience with learning, and as a result, they will be able to release the protective cocoons that have kept them from trying.

LOVE

Young people need to know that someone cares about them. They need to believe that their authentic selves are loveable—something they can only learn from being loved. They also need to know there are reasonable limits in life and what those limits are, because limits teach them that someone cares enough about them to help them be safe from both their own unbridled impulses and a scary world.

Real love is unconditional and should underlie all aspects of the relationship between parent and child. Real love is not dependent on a young person's obedience nor doled out only when a young person earns it. It cannot be taken away because of a poor performance on an athletic field or a test. It is motivated by a genuine, internal desire to do what is best for the young person, not what is most advantageous or satisfying for the adult. Children and teenagers need to know unequivocally that their parents love them, despite the day-to-day difficulties in their young lives.

Students who lack adequate love experiences at home need to learn about love from us (Glasser, 1969, p. 13). We, too, can care about them unconditionally, despite their failures and disruptive behaviors. We can communicate to them that we value them, believe they can succeed, and are willing to go side by side with them through their learning processes. We do this with our kindness.

I am not advocating laissez-faire teaching or "touchy-feely" classrooms with no substance. I believe in high standards and clear limits. What I am advocating, however, is that while we structure the experiences in our classrooms and respond to student behaviors, we also guide, even coach, our students to success, all the while showing them that we value them. We need to spend more time supporting our students, truly teaching them, and less time scrutinizing them and their work. It is important to note that scrutinizing and judging are qualitatively different from assessing. Assessing work in progress helps provide direction in how to proceed, but scrutinizing implies looking for faults. I was surprised at myself and discouraged when I first compared the amount of time I spent judging students to how much less time I spent working individually *with* them.

Working with a student is attending to her or him and thereby showing that student someone cares. Care, according to May, "is a particular type of intentionality" (1969, p. 292); it means that we "must do something about a situation" (p. 191). Students who have experienced very little love in their lives thirstily lap up the care and attention we pay them, right there in our classrooms. Some young people are very difficult to love. They push us away and/or do exactly what we want them not to do. However, these are the kids who need love the most (Brendtro et al., 1998, p. 78). Their cold, rejecting, or defiant behaviors are but defense mechanisms, carefully built up throughout the many years of their underloved lives.

"Courtney" was a difficult student for me to love. She was a popular senior at an upscale public school at which I taught. In class, she glared at me and listened to my instructional suggestions with her nose curled up in a snarl. When I finished talking, she quickly turned to her friends to gossip or "act cool." She was well dressed and acted elite, although she was also a bit overweight, masculine, and not at all pretty. I tried to avoid interacting her with as much as possible and gave her minimal help with her projects, because I did not like feeling rejected by her.

A few weeks into the semester, her mother came in for a routine conference. What a surprise! Her mother had been my high school French teacher. "Mademoiselle" had been and still was perfectly beautiful, svelte, impeccably dressed, and had every lock of her hair in order. She walked with poise and dignity and spoke with clear enunciation.

Our conference went smoothly, as Courtney was doing satisfactory work. Throughout the conference, however, I kept to myself memories of how Mademoiselle had been unkind and dishonest to me when I was her student. For days afterward, I pondered the stark contrast between beautiful Mademoiselle (now Madame) and her ugly-duckling daughter.

Then it hit me. How awful it must be for Courtney, awkward and plain, to look in the mirror and then at her mother. How inadequate she must feel, every single day. In addition, her mother must also be dishonest and unkind to her at times, as she had been to me. I began to have empathy for Courtney, instead of resentment. When I went to her table to help with her project, I sat down next to her, taking time to connect with her, looking into her eyes and smiling, whether or not she smiled back at me. As I treated her like a special member of my class, I became immune to her snarls, and before long they disappeared. Courtney warmed up, and we spent the rest of the semester in a cooperative teacher-student relationship. Of course, Courtney's classwork improved because her attitude improved. Her attitude improved because she believed I cared about her.

Psychologists are well aware that love is essential to human development. On his hierarchy of human needs, Abraham Maslow (1968) listed love and belonging as the third rung, just above basic sustenance and physical safety. Only after one's need for love is met, according to Maslow, is one able to give attention to the higher levels: self-esteem, self-actualization (which I believe includes motivation to learn), and transcendence. When people are unable to have their needs for love satisfied, their development is stymied and their energies are siphoned away from higher-level developmental activities, including education.

In their remarkable book *Reclaiming Youth at Risk: Our Hope for the Future*, authors Brendtro, Brokenleg, and Bockern (1998) propose methods for reaching difficult youth. These methods rely entirely on nurturing behaviors that counteract discouragement. Their theories are based on traditional Native American child-rearing practices and are described as "the circle of courage." Arranged according to the four sacred directions of Native American culture, the tenets are significance/belonging, competence/mastery, power/independence, and virtue/generosity. To Brendtro and colleagues, significance is the result of being loved and having a sense of belonging. It is "found in the acceptance, attention, and affection of others" (1992, p. 45). To emphasize the importance in difficult young lives of loving relationships with adults, they quote renowned psychiatrist Karl Menninger, who wrote, "Living with and loving other human beings who return that love is the most strengthening, salubrious emotional experience in the world" (cited in Brendtro et al., 1992,. p. 48).

Young people who lack the affirmation of being loved are often willing to sacrifice everything for peer acceptance. Gangs and pregnancy fill the empty spaces in the hearts of underloved teenagers because they seem to offer "someone who's got my back" and "someone who will love me." Sometimes a teenager will go to great lengths to find proof that he or she is really loved. "Rick's" story is an example.

Feeling unloved, Rick tested his parents, continually upping the ante in hopes that one day his parents would come through and prove they loved him.

He was in a specialized class for ninth-grade, potential dropouts in a middle-class suburban high school. He was warm and easy to like, somewhat attractive, and bright enough to succeed in school, but not doing so. My late husband, who was his teacher and track coach, gave Rick lots of attention in class and during practice. He and Rick developed a close teacher-student relationship and my husband worked very hard trying to help Rick overcome his problems. However, Rick kept getting himself into progressively worse trouble.

When my husband and I accepted a dinner invitation to his home, we noticed some clues that helped explain his behavior. His parents were overtly welcoming to us, amiable and outgoing, and talked continually about themselves and their own interests. The father, who was losing his hair, talked about his hairpiece and the mother, who presumably had healthy hair, talked about her wig. I couldn't ignore the symbolism of two people trying to literally put on appearances. Nor did I forget their egocentrism.

Rick was having success on the track team, which was something positive and hopeful in his life. Then, one day after a particularly good week at track, he lit up a cigarette in plain view of the coach. Of course my husband had to reprimand him, invoke the school antismoking policy, and administer the appropriate suspension from the team. Rick's blatant actions seemed difficult to comprehend in light of the success he was having on the track team.

As he continued high school, his behavior worsened. By his senior year, he had left his parent's home and was sleeping in an old barn on the back of someone's property. His parents' reaction was to nag him about why he was doing this to them. They admonished him not to come home until he was ready to behave.

Eventually, Rick enlisted in the Army. He asked my husband to go with him to the main intersection of town at 5:00 A.M., where the recruiting officer would pick him up and take him off to the service. His parents were angry he had deserted them for the Army and refused to condone his actions by seeing him off.

On the surface, Rick's parents seemed to be pleasant, caring people. They often called the teacher to ask after their son, they entertained the teacher, and acted interested in school. But Rick needed more. He needed them to respond to *him*, to recognize *him* as a valuable person, and to show up every day in *his* life as people who cared enough to pay attention to *him*. I believe that Rick engaged in progressively more dramatic and dysfunctional behaviors to get his parents to finally come and save him, to show him they loved him. As long as I was acquainted with him, they never did.

For some young people, getting in trouble in order to hook and reel in adult attention proves successful. Such attention-seeking behavior is sometimes also called "attachment behavior" because it is "the persistent effort to connect with others" (Brendtro et al., 1998, p. 73). Attention-seeking kids build a history of acting out because they know intuitively that getting in trouble is a sure-fire way to keep their parents and teachers actively—albeit unhappily—involved in their lives. As teachers, we need to be careful not to feed these kids' need for love with more negative attention. Instead, we should find ways to give steady doses of positive attention, thereby helping alleviate their need to engage in dysfunctional attention-getting behaviors. These young people need to experience the necessary pleasure of feeling valuable and interesting instead of the destructive satisfaction of at least being noticed.

What Can We Do about Love? Love and Model Love

Love is a loaded word. It can mean something as frivolous as loving peanut butter, as trite as a Valentine heart, as erotic as making love, as romantic as falling in love, or as life changing as truly caring for the welfare of another. The love I am discussing is the last kind. We love our students when we are willing to feel empathy for their situations and devote ourselves to their physical, intellectual, and emotional well-being.

Almost everyone who goes into the teaching profession has said that they "love kids." At age eighteen, or whenever someone first thinks about becoming a teacher, "loving kids" usually refers to the idealistic notion of kids: kids are cute, and we think they are going to love us back.

The impression that being with kids is going to be fun for us and satisfy our egos is what launches us into the profession. Real kids, however, are not like the ideal. Real love for another human being is not always what it's cracked up to be, either.

Love means caring about someone even during the hard times, even when he or she is a pain in the butt, even when *our* needs aren't being satisfied. Loving students is about what *they* need. Truly caring about and for someone else will give us vast rewards, too, but the focus of our energies needs to be on the student.

Now I'm not saying that each student's entire welfare is in our hands, nor should it be. But I am saying that a large portion of it is. A few minutes a day may seem small, but for some young people these few minutes have a major effect. Katharine, for instance, came from a whole family of art and literature specialists. She had never thought much about studying science or math, though in tenth grade biology class she was surprised to be enjoying her genetics lessons and finding them easy. Her future was changed when her math teacher said that even though she was earning Bs in his class, he had noticed how easily she was grasping the concepts. He took the time to notice her and how she thinks, then to communicate his observations to her. She began to believe that she could succeed in science and math and is now on the way to a career in medicine.

The effect of a little love on Jed's life was even more dramatic. He was a rowdy high school freshman with learning disabilities who often found himself in the disciplinary office. His favorite out-of-school activity was painting graphics on the racecars that he also drove. He envisioned himself as a future racecar mechanic. His teachers, including his special education resource teachers, were, at most, hopeful that he would eventually graduate.

Jed entered my beginning drawing class the semester my husband was succumbing to cancer; therefore, I was present in Jed's class only a few times that whole term. But, being a likeable guy who asked for a lot of positive reinforcement, he received much of my attention on the few days I was there. A year later we crossed paths in the hall. He was planning his schedule for his junior year and "kind of missed art." Though he believed that his drawing skills were mediocre at best, he asked me what courses I was teaching next year. I encouraged him to take the watercolor class, even if he had trouble drawing. I told him I would help him through.

After some lessons in manipulating water paint, it became obvious that Jed was a highly competent, realistic painter. He did not believe it at first, so I lavished on the praise, though I also called him an "anal retentive painter" because of the almost rigid detail in his work. But he became a star in the class. Gradually, his self-confidence grew. At the end of that class, he signed up to take the advanced placement (AP) art class his senior year.

Jed was not your typical AP student. His drawings were tight copies of objects rather than self-expressive works of art. He preferred linear pencil drawings to shaded or colored images. The proportions and details, however, were precise and intriguing. I began to see in Jed a talent very specific to the field of industrial design.

On an ordinary but life-changing day, an admissions representative from the Art Institute of Pittsburgh (AIP) visited our AP class. She did her PowerPoint presentation and handed out postcards to interested students. Much to my surprise, Jed was enthralled. In the days to come, he began to imagine himself going to college at the art institute. Jed, remember, was neither expected to go to college nor even to graduate from high school.

He has come back to visit me twice since he began his college career at AIP. He has been making superior grades and is a high achiever in the department of industrial design. He rattled off the names of several Web-based design projects on which he has been a collaborator, mentioned a project at Carnegie Mellon for which he is being interviewed, and told me of a meeting he has scheduled with an automaker to present one of his original designs. What thrilled me even more than Jed's accomplishments were the vitality and pride that he exuded as he told me about his college experiences.

Jed's life is an example of how creative growth can overcome the nagging forces of entropy. And it happened because of a little love. What I gave Jed was the small gift of caring enough about him to find his goodness and talent. But this little gift, like a treasure chest of possibilities, has opened to him an unpredicted array of joys and successes. To watch Jed's face as he talks to me now, to absorb his positive energy, to be the recipient of his grateful hug, are rewards that motivate me to keep trying—even on those tough days—to offer love to the blue jay students presently in my classes.

Love means giving. What we teachers can give is acknowledgment, acceptance, concern, knowledge, wisdom, and inspiration. We begin by paying real attention to what young people have to say, and by listening, truly listening. I base much of my teaching on the following wise quote, though I don't know who said it: "What kids these days need is a good listening to!" In response to a few inquisitive comments, students often become fountains of personal information. They are anxious for someone to hear the truth about their lives and the emotions they carry with them daily.

After the shootings at Columbine and other schools, many people asked why no one at school had any clues that the kids in question were full of such pain and violence. The clues were undoubtedly there, however, waiting for a perceptive adult to notice . . . as I found out.

Erik, who was in a special program for ninth-graders with school problems, also participated in the after-school art club I supervised. He winced when I offered him a hug at one of our meetings and later told me he had never in his life been hugged. Week after week he made bloody, horrid drawings of tortured bodies. When he discussed them, he explained about his unhappy home, his agonizing history of being bullied at school, and his parallel urges for violence and suicide. Years later, I learned that Erik's history, his violent imaginings, and his association of murder and suicide were all characteristics of the students who committed mass murder in their schools. Erik, however, never acted out his disturbing images and continued through a couple more years of school without a major incident. He is now twenty-three years old. He has designed his own website (how I located him again) where he publishes his and others' creative writing. He has also created many music CDs, has a serious girlfriend, and reports that his depressed days are over.

When he was still in school, he would stop in my room and show me his latest drawings and poems. I always asked and he always answered that he was all right as long as he could put his feelings on paper. I am grateful Erik found enough love in the art room and in his special classroom to guide him safely toward adulthood. I am glad I attended to the meaning in his creative work so he had someone standing next to him as he, page by page, expressed and released his anguish.

3.4. Untitled Drawing *by Erik Bosko, Student*

The point illustrated by Erik's story is that students are constantly dropping hints, hoping that we will notice and then ask them the hard questions that, finally, will allow them to share their troubling thoughts. We need to listen, then ask, then listen some more. Eventually, we can offer advice and knowledge, but only after they know we care (Benson, Williams, and Johnson, 1987). And there is no better way to let a young person know you care than to spend time listening to what he or she needs to communicate.

Real listening requires us to suspend both critical judgment and our adult need to preach. It means trying to hear the feelings and needs that lie beneath the self-protective cocoons of our students' language. It means being educated, ourselves, about mediation, mood disorders, learning styles, substance abuse, eating disorders, physical and sexual abuse, and developmental psychology so that we can understand the implications of what our students are revealing to us. It means having the courage to face with our students the painful experiences of their lives.

Students who suffer from lack of loving attention at home will be revitalized when we show that we truly care about them by truly hearing them. Love-starved kids will learn about love as we model it—as we give our time to them, openly accept their feelings, help them learn appropriate limits, and are present in their lives with them—even if only for a few minutes a day. We will both give love and teach love to them. What better way is there to change the world and counter entropy?

Spitzmueller and James wrote:

> as i ponder the events of the recent past, I ask what if we had seen the suffering of eric harris and dylan kleibold before the incident at columbine. what if we had . . . surfed to their web site, and seen the plans that were unfolding there, plans manifested as personal and communal destruction. what if we had viewed their blueprints not as a scheme for destroying life, but as an expression of how their lives were being destroyed as they lived, as they endured the pain of their existence within a community that could not understand what moved them. what if we had seen that within these boys there was a thwarted drive to manifest itself in a way that could not be contained by their families and peers, the suburban pipe dream in which they were fated to live. what if we had noticed that there was more to them than just bad kids—kids gone wrong. what if we hadn't judged them, but shown them compassion . . . what if the community had been able to accommodate the diversity that was present within it. (2002, p. 125)

EMPOWERMENT

Opportunities to be an independent and competent agent in the world result in a sense of empowerment. Many believe that empowerment is a basic human need (Erikson, 1950; Oremus, 2004). Too little freedom can force kids to rebel in order to have some autonomy. Too much freedom without guidance can result in kids who are independent but dysfunctional, for they have not been taught how to use their freedom responsibly. Freedom without responsibility is not empowerment; empowerment is the ability to act *successfully* on one's own. Problems with empowerment at home and in school may lead to both self-destructive and aggressive tendencies in students.

Young people with few opportunities to take charge of their own lives and make their own decisions are often afraid of the world (Brendtro et al., 1998) because they are not learning how to manage themselves. Others engage in extreme experiences because they are so hungry for freedom that they overindulge. Do we not all know of the "perfect" son or daughter in high school who started college and seemed to go crazy when suddenly confronted with freedom? Now that the iron fists of home and school have let go, what capabilities has the child developed to supervise himself or herself? Such young people are not motivated so much by a desire to rebel against home as they are frantically fulfilling a craving for autonomy. The costs of too little empowerment can be high.

Some of our students deal with deficits of independence by turning on themselves. There is an epidemic of eating disorders that can be related to adolescent needs for autonomy. Some young people who are starving themselves to death due to anorexia nervosa are exercising the only control of their lives that they can: control over what they eat. While there are many other factors related to eating disorders, control is a major one.

Students who are overcontrolled by adults and lack a sense of empowerment are often perfectionists. They are plagued with constant feelings of inadequacy no matter how excellent their work. They are never good enough to meet the unattainable expectations of the powerful adults in their lives and are not free enough to set realistic expectations and goals for themselves. In addition, they may be burning their candles at both ends to achieve goals imposed on them by significant adults, all the while neglecting their true interests and gifts. Many of my students have told me that they are forced and sometimes paid by their parents to participate in sports they no longer enjoy or to plan business or medical careers that relegate their most authentic creative gifts to hobbies.

Rather than turning against themselves, some students deal with their lack of empowerment by fighting tooth and nail for it. They argue (with a capital A), break rules for seemingly no reason, walk out of the house or the classroom, refuse to study, insist on doing things their way, pierce and tattoo their bodies, live on the edge, and push us away as aggressively as possible. Sometimes they engage in dangerous behaviors such as drug abuse, binge drinking, casual sex, and crime in order to prove to themselves that they have control over their own lives. They rebel voraciously.

Basing their definition of empowerment on their negative life and school experiences, blue jay students with empowerment issues often believe that empowerment means "someone who has power to do things to you" (Oremus, 2004). As a result, they rebel against those who have power over them and aggressively exert power over other, weaker individuals. According to Oremus, kids who are denied empowerment "will go for any kind of control available, i.e. class clown, talk back, bad behavior . . . they will engage in self-defeating behavior . . . just to have some kind of control" (2004).

Too much independence has negative consequences, as well. Kids with too much autonomy crave limits in their lives. "Michael" is an example. His parents were asked to attend a staff conference because Michael, an obviously intelligent ninth-grader, was doing poorly in school. His main deficits were in completing homework assignments and finishing in-class work on time. His parents talked redundantly about his high intelligence and how emphatically they did not want to inhibit his talents. Apparently, his mother's parents had caused her much pain by oppressing her talents, and she, therefore, was not going to commit the same crime against her son. Instead, she committed the opposite one. Michael's parents never pressured him to do his homework, declined to direct or redirect his activities, and left him physically and emotionally alone for long hours. He spent his young life as he pleased. Daily, he stayed home by himself late into the evenings while his parents worked, turning to his computer for companionship. At the school conference, his parents unabashedly reported that, instead of doing his homework, he spent up to four hours a day on the computer communicating with his twenty-three-year-old Internet girlfriend. Michael's parents did not question the validity of this girlfriend nor let themselves recognize the danger of Michael's Internet love life. Neither did they accept responsibility to encourage him to do his schoolwork. In fact, whenever teachers at the conference tried to counsel the parents into creating some limitations for Michael's own good, they parried by reenforcing their own pain and refusal to do anything that might inhibit their son. Michael's story did eventually adopt a positive ending. As his high school career went on, he responded immediately to those of his teachers who offered him a combination of attention and clear expectations. He began to value his schoolwork and to engage in after-class conversations with those adults he was beginning to trust.

I first experienced evidence that a young person needs limits in his or her life to feel secure when my daughter, Yvonne, was not quite three. She was engaging in some (now-forgotten) unacceptable behavior, so her father sent her to her room. As she stomped off, she turned to him and, with all the vehemence a three-year-old could muster, said, "You're a terrible daddy" and then slammed her door. Of course her dad and I were horrified. After a ten-minute cooling-down period, however, she emerged from her room and gave her daddy a big hug. There may be several interpretations of this event, but what I learned from it was that underneath the defensiveness of her anger, she appreciated knowing that her Daddy loved her enough to give her life boundaries.

We raised our daughter to lead herself, to be autonomous; we gave her choices, self-determination, and opportunities to express her true, creative self. We also gave her boundaries and reenforced them. Years later, the net result is a young woman who can take care of herself in almost any situation but who also carefully balances her autonomy with a respect for the rights and needs of others.

Our students, too, need chances to practice responsible autonomy and, when necessary, to be taught how to lead themselves in functional and constructive ways. We can offer them those chances in our classrooms and schools, but we must also stand next to them and help them learn how to use autonomy responsibly.

What Can We Do about Empowerment?
Give Students Choices, Responsibilities, and Guidance

For young people to practice autonomy, they should be given opportunities to make choices and help in deciding. When they make mistakes, they will need guidance to recognize and deal with the subsequent real consequences of their actions. This way, young people will have frequent but guided chances to learn to be in charge of their own lives.

Instead of teaching empowerment, schools often present either rigid and unattainable expectations for student behavior or too few bound-

aries within which to operate. Either way, students are expected to figure out on their own how to live competently and responsibly.

As teachers, we can create situations that help students learn independence. This may require some adjustments in our teaching styles,
because we will need to relax our control of the classroom and ask students to direct more of their own learning situations. How can we do
that? Students can't lead themselves! However, if we do not teach them
how to be self-directed, then when and from whom are they going to
learn it? Our blue jay students, as we have already discussed, are missing knowledge about how to manage their lives, choices, emotions, and
interactions. That is why they are having trouble in school. What life
skills they do have were likely learned from dysfunctional parents, siblings, and/or peers. Our blue jays need the other adults in their lives—
us—to help them learn how to live and succeed.

Because many of our students are inexperienced at self-directed learning, we can start small. For instance, having students make their own
choices about topics for papers, creative writing assignments, or science
experiments enables them to self-direct their learning in small ways.
Having them determine deadlines and consequences for missing them is
another example.

As students learn to lead themselves, we can increase their free-
dom/responsibility. We can become learning guides rather than mere
dispensers of information by changing the structure of our information
delivery systems. Instead of lecturing, we can introduce a unit of study;
provide resources, time, and academic questions; then set the kids free
in the classroom to find the answers themselves. Some students will get
right to work and stay very busy. We can let them be. Other students
will try to use the time as a "blow-off" or be unsure of how to start. We
can go to them and teach them to set small, attainable goals. We can sit
down next to them and show them how to learn. We can give them lots
of positive reenforcement for trying and accomplishing whatever they
are able to do.

We need some limits, as well. So we assess their daily effort and require that they demonstrate their newly acquired knowledge. Of course
we will have been sitting side by side with our students and coaching
them, so we will know that they have been learning. These demonstra-
tions of knowledge can be adapted to a variety of learning styles. Some

students might choose to write papers, others to prepare audio or video-tapes on which they recite or present their new knowledge; some may wish to do illustrated reports. We can also provide opportunities for self-assessment. This way they will learn to make judgments about their own performances, to identify their own strengths and areas for improvement. We should, then, make a big deal to the whole class about how everyone engaged in independent learning—picked their own resources, set their own goals, and evaluated their own performances. We might even talk about how well they used their freedom; kids love to feel they have freedom.

Through authentic learning experiences, we can show our difficult students how freedom is balanced with responsibility. Instead of asking them to sit passively and absorb all the information we are prescribing for them, we can ask them to think of the "big questions" and teach them to research and ponder the answers themselves. We can have them choose their own study topics or writing assignments and teach them how to think creatively. We can make them responsible for helping determine the rules of the classroom and also determine the consequences to be imposed for breaches. We can remind them that we trust them to evaluate themselves and to help each other learn. We can give them guided experiences with autonomy and teach them to live empowered lives.

They will need us there to hold their hands for a while, as they learn to be successful, autonomous agents in the world. My mother says that I could walk before I was quite a year old, but that for months afterward I had at least one finger touching the edge of something. Venturing out into the world must have felt much safer if I had just a touch of support to guide me.

So I recommend that we begin to transform our classrooms from geometrically arranged stations for teacher-controlled activity to busy environments for students to gradually, then vigorously, practice self-leadership. We will still be important figures to our students because we are authorities in our fields and mature people with accrued wisdom (Glasser, 1992, p. 54). Our jobs will become more satisfying because we will no longer have to drive our students like cattle to try to get them to learn. Instead, we will be teaching them how to lead themselves and become independent, empowered learners.

Empowerment should be a goal of our teaching. The director of a preschool where I worked taught me, "You'll know you have been successful when your students don't need you anymore." We can get students to this point by helping them find their creative and constructive abilities, by teaching students how to use them for the greater good, and by showing students that they are important enough to go into the world and actualize their gifts. Even the blue jays have gifts, and they need the most help becoming empowered to use them.

THE RELATIONSHIP BETWEEN LOVE AND EMPOWERMENT

Developmental psychologists have identified several stages of intellectual and emotional development that all people progress through as they grow up. As teachers, our job becomes much easier if we are aware of the developmental stages of our students. One of the most useful statements I have ever heard uttered about children's development was said by Dr. Lendon Smith on a television talk show in the 1970s. He told parents that to deal with "the terrible two's" they should realize these children are practicing for adolescence. At the time, I was a high school teacher and my children were toddlers. I heard him loud and clear!

Two-year-olds have grown up enough so they can get around on their own, speak their wishes, affect their environments, and play without help. They are learning about possession and self-expression. They seem willful and stubborn because they are trying to become people who can function separately from Mommy and Daddy. It is their job to learn to do this. But every time two-year-olds walk away from or defy Mom or Dad, they also know that they are separating from Mom and Dad and may be displeasing them. This is frightening and sad. Life for a two-year-old is a constant tug of war, trying to become autonomous without alienating parents and shaming oneself (Erikson, 1950). Piaget (1975) calls this a stage of "disequilibrium," the very impetus for growth.

Teens and preteens are in a similar disequilibrium. They are trying very hard to gain independence in their lives, as we have already discussed. They want to drive a car, explore their sexuality, test their athletic potential, make their own decisions, pierce their own bodies, and follow their dreams. It is their job to become independently competent people, to be empowered to live successfully.

Along with independence, however, comes the threat of isolation, so they are also working very hard to develop and maintain loving relationships with adults and peers. Loving and being loved is essential at all ages but takes on new dimensions as one grows in independence. There are risks. After all, if Mom and/or Dad have always been there to feed a young person, shelter, nurse, and bail him or her out of trouble, it feels like a big risk to grow up. But it is also unbearable not to.

Our older students are in developmental disequilibrium and sometimes make our lives—and theirs—miserable just because they are trying to establish love and independence in their lives. Those who struggle the most trying to get their love and independence needs balanced will often engage in extreme behaviors.

Psychologists know that children who are abused tend to grow into one of two adult roles: victim or aggressor (B. Moon, June 1993, personal communication). Similarly, students without a comfortable balance of love and independence internalize the same roles. Some of the students, and I believe these are the most at risk, deal with these deficits in their lives by turning on themselves, and being their own victims. They skip school, punish themselves with eating disorders and depression, self-mutilate, or take drugs to anesthetize their pain. They erode themselves from the inside out in order to actualize their beliefs that they must be inadequate and, therefore, unworthy of the love, security, and freedom that others seem to have.

Some students take on the aggressor role. They hate, they hurt others, they mouth off, they live on the edge to frighten or anger the adults in their lives. They push us away as aggressively as possible in hopes we will go after them to show them we care or to prove to themselves they have independence.

I believe the common wisdom that teens always rebel is a myth. Teens absolutely need to differentiate from the adults in their lives in order to find and establish themselves as people in their own rights. This trip to a differentiated self takes place on a bumpy road full of power-struggles, mistakes, limit testing, and depression sessions. These are to be expected. But aggressive or self-destructive extremes of behavior, I believe, are really symptoms of empowerment and love gone awry. Far too

often, adults fail to intervene in kids' lives or to adjust their own ineffective methods because they mistakenly believe "it's normal for kids to
rebel." Healthy maturation occurs only within an environment that offers both empowerment and love.

NOTE

1. More information about learning styles and differentiated teaching is
available in *A Mind at a Time* by Mel Levine (2002) and through the Coalition
of Essential Schools, www.essentialschools.org

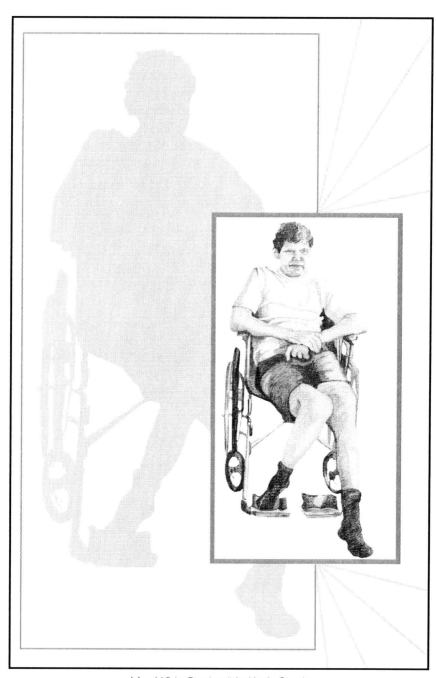

4.1. M.S. in October II *by Nicole Gnezda*

4

IT MATTERS HOW WE TREAT DIFFICULT KIDS

When I was young, my mother told me, "We should stand back in awe of the mystery of every person we meet." I wasn't quite sure what she meant, then, but I get it now. It is my firm belief that each and every human is born important, even though the importance is often hard to perceive. Sometimes it is hidden so very deeply and under so many layers of cocoon protection that it never sees the light of day. But I know that every person, in his and her essence, matters greatly. I know this because of Walt.

Walt was my father. With prominent cheekbones, a strong forehead, wavy hair that never grayed, and perfect teeth, Walt was handsome. His height was six foot two, though I have few memories of him standing. My father had Multiple Sclerosis (MS).

They say that all the way back to his college days he had symptoms and when I became a part of the family, he had already been rejected from a second tour in the Navy. He was diagnosed five years later—the same year my brother was born. My mother says she spilled tears all over my brother for the first two weeks of his life. Three years later, Daddy could no longer hold a job.

When he walked, he stumbled with leg braces and noisy metal crutches. He fell down a lot in public, and often no one helped him get up again. He lost his ability to write, and his eyesight became so weak that he could no longer read. He subscribed to Books-on-Tape and joked that though *Playboy* was boring, "it might be fun in Braille." He used to ask me to scratch his nose and move his legs. Our neighbor Darrell would come over to help him go to the toilet. When I went away to college, Dad was bed-ridden, and later, in his final years, he could hardly speak.

In his whole adult life, my father achieved nothing. He did not have an impressive job title. He did not make a good living. He did not publish, invent, establish a charity, or run for office. His life fit into the boundaries of our house where he stayed in his bed until, in 1980, he died at the age of fifty-three.

However, my father was the most important person in our family. We never had a birthday without him at the table or a Christmas morning without him lying on the family room sofa. He knew everything that was happening in our government, could do complex math problems in his head, and would help out other MS patients via the telephone. When I came home he was always there to listen, to counsel me, or just to nap next to. We knew our father better than almost any kid in the 1950s knew his or her dad, and we loved him immensely. The greatest gift my mother gave us was to keep him home, out of a nursing home, with our family.

What I learned from my father's disabled life was that the value of a human being is not dependent upon his or her achievements, successes, attractiveness, social status, talent, popularity, or fame. A person is valuable simply because she or he exists in our world.

This important lesson was reenforced in my life two more times. When I was in labor with my first child and the contractions felt as powerful as a Mack truck, I thought about the importance of life. And when my daddy died, slowly, laboring with every ratchetlike breath, I realized it again. I decided that if coming into the world and going out of it take such enormous physical and emotional effort, then being alive must be very, very important, indeed.

This is true for everyone! Not just our A students and the ones who follow our rules. The drug-addicted, belligerent, pregnant, hyperactive, and unlovable students in our midst have as much value as everyone else.

When we walk into our classrooms knowing this, our attitudes toward our students change. The difficult students stop being our "problem students" and start being our challenges. We begin to look deeper than their protective cocoons to find the sparkling spirits that lie hidden beneath. In our students' screeching and chattering we hear the sound and remember the color of the blue jay. We stop labeling our difficult students, aggravating their maladies, and exacerbating their defenses. We begin, instead, to love them.

Once I bought a copy of an adage attributed to St. Francis DeSales printed on handmade paper. It says, "There is nothing so strong as gentleness and nothing so gentle as real strength." My students have taught me the meaning: Love, gentleness, is what changes lives. The power we have to bring our students to a place where they can learn and succeed, also gives us the power to teach them that they are valuable.

Our difficult students don't walk into class with clanging metal crutches, like Walt; theirs are carefully disguised. These students are not suffering from a slow deterioration of the nervous system, but a deterioration of the spirit. When they fall down, are we going to do nothing because we, like the people who saw my father fall, are put off, or are afraid to get involved, or don't know what to do?

What we can do is be truly present with our blue jays, sit down next to them, and treat them like they are worth a million bucks. We can listen to whatever they have to say, suspending judgment and hearing the clues about who they really are. Then we will know what they need and how to reach them, and they will begin to trust us enough to reach back. Little by little, miracles will happen. The same student who was "impossible" when confronted with the brute forces of rules and criticism will be softened and made pliable by the magic of gentleness. We can be patient, open, aware, and amazed. We can be more successful teachers than we have ever been before. I know it will happen. I have seen many lives change because of the true strength of gentleness and the power of unconditional love. Let's try it with each and every difficult student because, as Alec Baldwin iterated in the movie *Prelude to a Kiss* (Rene, 1992), "Never to be squandered, the miracle of another human being."

5.1.   Cosmos *by Nicole Gnezda*

5

IT'S ALL ABOUT THE SOIL: A PARABLE

It was the first year to plant a garden in the yard of my new house. I had a lovely ravine in the back, shaded with age-old wild cherry trees and accompanied by a gurgling creek. In the front yard there was sun, sun, sun. This was the place for flowers! So I planted. Along the right edge of the yard I emptied six bags of fresh topsoil, spaded it, and mixed it with peat moss. For a couple of days I even marveled at the beauty and scent of the plain, umber earth. Along the road in the front of the house was a country-style wooden mailbox on a post. I spaded around it, too. No topsoil or peat moss here, I just wanted to get it planted. In both gardens I placed a variety of seeds, including those long and lanky cosmos—the ones in the movie *A Color Purple* (Spielberg, 1985) that God liked so much.

I waited, checking the garden each day, and finally saw sprouts. Day by day, the sprouts grew, lengthening into the sky—the ones on the side of the house at least did. The cosmos around the mailbox sort of "pooped out": they grew to be only fifteen inches high and squeezed out a few short-lived blossoms.

My daughter Yvonne, now a landscape architect's assistant, came home for a visit. I proudly showed off my garden: the tomatoes, the daisies, and the elegant cosmos. Then I sadly showed her my mailbox cosmos. She said, "Um hmm," laughed, and added, "It's all about the soil, Mom. It's all about the soil."

6.1.   Untitled Sculpture *by Callie Herman, Student*

6

RECONSIDERING ASSUMPTIONS: CLEANING OUT OUR BRAINS

From the day we entered our first classroom as a teacher, we have been hauling on our backs loads of assumptions about students and teaching. Many are stereotypes, labels, and common pieces of wisdom that we have assimilated into our worldviews without doing much thinking. Now it is time to look at these assumptions with a critical eye.

ABOUT AUTHORITY AND RESPECT

"Kids don't respect their elders anymore." "I demand respect in my classroom." "You have to earn my respect." "Kids these days have a problem with authority." "Question authority." Wow! Respect and authority sure get a lot of lip service, but I'm not certain that they are understood very well.

The word "authority" has commonalties with "authoritative," "author," "and " "authoritarian." In their most positive usage, "authority" and related words describe the vastness and esteem of one's knowledge, such as "Dr. Lewis is an *authority* on the subject of genetics." These words give credibility by establishing critical acceptance of a body of knowledge, as in "*Webster's Unabridged* is the *authoritative* text on pronunciation." They can also imply the origin of information, knowledge, or thought: for example, "Jung *authored* the theory of the collective subconscious.". In some cases, authority is used to refer to a bureaucratic organization that has a complete knowledge base and overarching responsibility for a system, such as the "Port Authority." In its more pejorative role, the concept of authority can be used as a euphemism for dictator. Some people are *authoritarians*; they make all the rules and impose all of the consequences. They run tight ships and expect blind submission.

How each one of us defines authority has critical impact on the quality of the learning in our classrooms because it determines the effectiveness of the relationships we build or do not build with our students. The old adage "Don't smile until Christmas" is derived from an underlying belief that to relate positively to young people means we will sacrifice our power to control them. Only after we have displayed our iron fists will our students "respect our authority" and behave for us. This disciplinary method is as old as horse-drawn carriages and one-room schoolhouses, but our students are two centuries more independent than those the method was made for.

Being a control freak may give us the illusion that things in the classroom will go the way we want them to, but it will, in fact, trigger the opposite responses from many kids. There are three reasons why.

1. A learning situation that is tightly controlled by an adult allows a student no room to express herself in the class. A student hungry for empowerment sees virtually one option: not to obey. Not obeying is establishing one's self as a person who is free to make choices, to be in charge of one's life, and to practice autonomy.

2. A student hungry to be cared about and have his or her self-worth validated may perceive one option in a tightly controlled classroom: to be a people-pleaser and follow all the rules in anticipation of praise. The results of this choice are ultimately empty because, in the end, the student has exhibited only an artificial self. She or he still will not know if the real self is interesting, loveable, and valuable. In this case, the student may eventually feel the need to act out and disobey the rules in order to express her or his individual self. Students who have been repeatedly rejected by

the adults in their lives may skip the stage of obedience altogether and reject the authoritarian teacher right off the bat, before the teacher can reject them.

3. The student who is not equipped with knowledge of how to learn in his or her strongest mode, how to interact appropriately in the classroom, and why the classroom rules exist, will flounder and seem erratic. Teaching students about individualized learning styles, good manners, and the reasons underlying rules will enable them to make sense of what is happening in the classroom and teach them to evaluate their own behaviors accordingly. Their behavior will not be hit or miss and they will not have to try to make sense of a teacher's classroom through trial and error. These students may be very willing to function within the system of a classroom if they could only figure it out.

"Don't smile until Christmas" and other highly teacher-controlled approaches set up an authoritarian system of control in school, a system destined to collapse into chaos or erupt into mayhem. In our schools, we see constant examples of chaotic and explosive behaviors. Sometimes their occurrence is limited to student-only environments like locker areas or weekend parties. Other times the mayhem breaks out blatantly in tragic school violence.

Instead, shouldn't we choose creative growth for our classrooms, basing our authority on expertise in our fields, on positive interpersonal relationships, and effective pedagogy? We can win our students over with our great minds, great personalities, and great hearts, without having to resort to authoritarianism to get and keep our students' attention. Who will not be impressed with all that we know? Who will not be impressed with the vitality of our true selves? Who will not be impressed with our kindness and interest? And once students are impressed with us, they will work for us, learn from us, and treat us kindly, too. They will respect us for our authority on academics and life.

We all want to be respected by our students. Respect means the valuing of someone, plain and simple. Submission to one's rules may seem like respect on the surface. Using proper forms of address and avoiding impolite vocabulary may also seem like respect, as well as being on time and "ready to go." But true respect lies much deeper than the surface behaviors that show it. It occurs naturally because someone honestly admires and values someone else.

Young people are very adept at testing us. They expect us to prove ourselves to them and are quite clear about wanting adults to earn their respect. Aren't we like that with our peers and our students as well? We respect the people whose values and accomplishments we admire and who treat us compassionately. So if we really want respect from our students we must be admirable, accomplished, and compassionate people. We must treat everyone with respect first.

The number-one rule in my classroom and my life is try to treat every person in ways that acknowledge his or her innate importance. We can be angry, frustrated, and disappointed, but we must also be caretakers of each others' dignity. This is respect. Young people will latch on to adults who treat them with this kind of respect and will respect them back. Once a classroom is established on the foundation of mutual respect, then no one—student or teacher—will need to fight for protection autonomy, to understand, or to feel valuable.

Authoritarians expect blind obedience and, at best, get a blind, unexamined, meaningless adherence to rules, motivated by the desire to avoid punishment or rejection. Authoritarianism breeds power-struggles and fear; it breeds entropy. However, if *authorities* offer students opportunities for independence within a curriculum, real affection from a shared relationship of true selves, and the kindness of explanations and help rather than punishments, then the authorities get to experience their students' growth, and their own. The brains grow and the hearts grow through positive teacher-student relationships. This is the creativity that counteracts entropy.

ABOUT COMPETITION

There is a belief among both educators and the public at large that competition in the classroom is a great academic motivator. In a discussion about competition in education, a former high school tailback once philosophized to me, "The harder the battle, the sweeter the victory." I agree whole-heartedly when I'm watching a game from the stands. But when it comes to school, I also ask myself, how sour is the loss for the others?

Comparing one student to another on a regular basis causes school failure instead of promoting learning. How? Imagine the embarrassment of the child stumbling over syllables, trying to read aloud to the class after others have read fluently. Or the frustration of the teen who fails a pop quiz about the novel he tried so hard to read at home, when the quiz seemed easy to his classmates. Or the humiliation of my son who was laughed at when he asked questions about math that others already understood. Or the peer pressure on the bright, hard-working student who is accused by her peers of "ruining the curve" with her strong performance on a test. Do any of us keep on trying to do those things that are painful or at we which we continue to fail?

All children begin life as good learners: they teach themselves to walk, talk, and play long before they get to school. If what happens to them in school nurtures them, builds up their self-worth, and gives them gratification, then they—the victors—will continue their winning school behaviors.

But the blue jays? In a competitive classroom, they become the losers who receive poor grades and frequent criticism and are "shown up" by students for whom learning comes more easily. When we adults are not good at a sport or hobby, we can quit and find another one. An academic loser, however, cannot always find another school (although some excellent alternative programs are beginning to emerge). She or he can quit trying, though. The student can pretend she or he doesn't care, fail on purpose, become a rebel, or stop coming to school altogether. Competition in the classroom may motivate some students to excel, but it also motivates many to give up.

Track and field is a different sort of sport from the football game played by my acquaintance, because it has a different kind of competition. Track and field is considered to be an "individual sport" because each athlete alone represents his or her team. While teams eventually win or rank in a team competition, the real victories occur one event, one athlete at a time.

Each athlete strives to consistently improve his or her individual performance, knowing that even a sixth place will score points. The athletes focus on their particular strengths, work to improve their areas of weakness, and set their sights on achieving their best performance to date, or their "personal record" (PR).

6.2. Competition *by Nicole Gnezda*

The following story is true; it happened several years ago to a boy on my late husband's team. It illustrates the significance of a PR.

"Kurt" had transferred from another school after being removed from a physically abusive home and placed with a foster family in our district. He was lanky and clumsy, pale skinned and red-haired. He walked with the stoop of someone who felt lowly and spoke with the stammer of insecurity.

It's a mystery to me why he even tried out for the track team, but he did. He became a two-miler. The two-mile is a long and grueling race, requiring eight laps around the track. Kurt would stumble around those laps, well behind a mob of other runners. At every meet, all the two-milers would finish, warm down, and get a drink. Kurt, far behind, would walk off the track, never finishing a race. The coach gave Kurt much encouragement and taught his teammates to respect him. Kurt kept coming to the meets, starting the races, and giving up.

One ordinary afternoon, our team was hosting Kurt's former school. When it was time for the two-mile race to begin, Kurt lined up with the pack of other runners. He started his race, clodding around the track, huffing, and grunting, as sweat dripped down his white, clammy skin. He was, again, considerably behind the rest of the runners as they began to cross the finish line. Pretty soon they had all finished the race.

For some reason, Kurt did not quit running that day. He just kept on clomping one foot after the other. His teammates took notice. They began to cheer for him. There were still several laps left for Kurt to go. He kept on running. They cheered. He ran. And for the first time in his life, he finished a race. His whole team yelled out as he came to the finish line. The team from his former school began to cheer for him as well, and then the people in the stands stood up and gave him an ovation.

Kurt was the star that day, but not because he won a trophy or because he was better than anyone else. Kurt was extremely slow and had finished dead last. However, losing the race was not sour at all. Instead, Kurt achieved a very important PR. With the encouragement of his teammates, he fought the enormous forces of entropy in his life and achieved something outstanding for him.

Competition was not the motivator for Kurt. Support from his teammates, good individualized instruction from his coaches, and a spirit still willing to try were his motivators. His success was not related to anyone else's success or failure, but it was great, and his victory was the sweetest of all.

ABOUT INTRINSIC MOTIVATION

Why did Kurt persist against great odds? It was not for the prize at the end of the race, nor a paycheck, nor a good grade; he never expected the crowd to cheer for his last-place finish. His motivation came from somewhere deep inside. Somewhere in his spirit was the desire to be better than he had been, to achieve a personal record. Maybe he had a seed of belief in his own worth, and maybe it had been fertilized by his coach's encouragement. Maybe he had too much pride to walk off the track in front of his former classmates. Maybe all of these factors pushed him to keep on running this time, past the period of pain, until he reached a "runner's high." I do not know. But one thing I do know is that his motivation for finishing his big race was intrinsic.

Intrinsic motivation is an integral part of positive growth because it entices one to create, to learn more, to perform better, and to help others. It comes from an internal sense of self-worth, of integrity, and of valuing life, and it brings great intrinsic rewards. Pride, self-esteem, gratification from doing one's best, the pleasure of helping others, and a "natural high" flourish within the individual as a result of meaningful work well done.

Researchers Teresa Amabile and Alfie Kohn conducted separate studies regarding intrinsic and extrinsic motivation. In Amabile's (1983) study, people were coaxed by extrinsic incentives to engage in creative tasks. She found that average people were motivated to produce some work, though not of high creative quality, and that highly creative people were negatively impacted by the offer of rewards. Kohn (1993) published an entire book, *Punished by Rewards*, that systematically denounces the use of extrinsic motivation in schools.

As teachers, we probably understand the concepts of intrinsic motivation and rewards. What is harder to understand, however, is why so many students seem to lack them.

I believe it is because our capitalistic society focuses too much on the extrinsic and too little on internal human qualities. Therefore, young people are rarely taught about the intrinsic. Our television sets and movie theaters ennoble material possession. Tanklike automobiles, mansion-sized houses, "cutting edge" fashions, even expensive underwear have become symbols of happiness that are projected into our children's eyes and psyches. Society's idols are either admired because of their wealth (Donald Trump, Bill Gates) or are lavished with wealth because of their popularity (professional athletes, movie stars). Our society awards high salaries to those individuals who already amass wealth and leaves to struggle those who devote their lives to professions that serve to help others. As we know, social workers, teachers, child and elderly care workers, and nurses are overworked and underpaid.

Our children grow up believing that big salaries, showy possessions, and impressive job titles are the markers of human success and happiness. What is more, schools have been reenforcing this belief system by using grades, awards, special privileges, and tokens to motivate children to learn. Nevertheless, when they show up in our classrooms, we expect our young people to suddenly value learning for learning's sake and bemoan the fact that many of them do not.

The pitfalls of an extrinsic approach to teaching affect every single student. Successful students learn to work only as much, or study as little, or inquire as only deeply as necessary to achieve the reward. Students who rarely receive the rewards often give up trying at all.

The good news is that we can affect changes in our students' values. We can teach them about intrinsic motivation by having them talk about personal integrity, true heroism, the internal satisfaction of hard work, the joy of self-expression, and the meaning of compassion. We can help them achieve personal records in our classrooms so they may begin to feel the intrinsic rewards for their hard work.

We can also resist the temptation to rely on teaching methods that feed greed-based motivation. We can set up learning problems for students to work through, rather than spoon-feeding them quantities of facts to repeat on tests. Their abilities to think will be validated. We can be by their sides as they go step by step through the learning process instead of assuming that long homework papers will teach them. They will be guided to the joy of success. We can assign creative work such as developing scientific hypotheses or original poetry instead of having them always studying someone else's. They will believe that their ideas matter.

We can treat grades as honest, criteria-based assessments instead of carrots to motivate compliance. Our students will learn to recognize their own strengths and improve their performances. We can value the efforts our students make to learn, to sustain their work process, to figure out their own ways of learning, and to help each other succeed. They will learn to value themselves and others. We can refuse to believe in the bell curve and help all students to achieve PRs. They will love being in our classes. They will learn to love learning.

Let us run side by side with all the Kurts in our classrooms and help them to finish. Then, we can applaud their efforts and ask them about their feelings of satisfaction. This way we will be valuing PRs, promoting intrinsic rewards, and cheering for *everyone's* growth.

ABOUT PROBLEM STUDENTS

I was walking through the halls of my high school one afternoon, accompanied by a gaggle of art students. Our purpose was, first, to view all of the art reproductions displayed around the building and then to write essays about them. We encountered the hall monitor. Though it was obvious this was a class engaged in educationally appropriate strolling, he made one of those all-too-common teacher-jokes about us not having hall passes. After I claimed responsibility for the kids, he continued the joke, "Oh. Do you have any problem students?" For him, this question was lightweight and somewhat funny. For me it wasn't.

The term "problem students" brings with it several implicit subtexts. It assumes in the first place that there are such things as problem students. Then it implies that *young people* are the teacher's problems, and that they are somehow defective. And it shifts responsibility for ameliorating the problem from us as educators (who could and should help all of our students) to children and adolescents who are already deeply wounded by the complexity of their lives' demands.

The real problem with problem students, perhaps, is that they create problems for *us*. They make our jobs more complicated: they question our authority, they upset our carefully ordered lesson plans, they make us question our adequacy as teachers, and they force us to develop relationships with them in order to teach them.

They also make us feel things we do not wish to feel. Teaching would be so much easier if we could just stay with our intellects, but difficult students can make us angry and scared. We get angry because they upset our sense of order, risk our self-esteem, take away our power, and cause us to lose composure in front of other people. They make us scared because they might hurt us, complain to their parents about us, keep us from covering the content we need to in order for our other students to pass standardized tests, and tell the principal or announce publicly that we are poor teachers.

I have found that young people have a gift for knowing exactly what to say to make an adult hurt the most ("You're a terrible daddy"). They also make us afraid that we might have to deal with situations we do not want to know about: sexual abuse, suicide, alcoholism, eating disorders, gangs, drugs, and pregnancy—to name some biggies. We know how to react to students in the way that hurts the most, too: we blame them for being wounded and not knowing how to get better.

Problems are not always bad, though. Creativity is sometimes defined as problem solving, as is math. Problems are really interesting dilemmas. When we are solving one we get to be a detective, a diagnostician, and an adventurer—sometimes a creative genius. Know how good it feels to fill in the last blank square in a crossword puzzle? Well, it feels a thousand times better to help a young person see his or her behavior as a problem to be solved, to encourage his or her self-knowledge and self-worth, and to guide the student to the resource people he or she needs to make his or her life satisfying and successful.

Yes, problem students do present problems in our classrooms. But just as a football player is more than a jock and a blue jay is more than its squawk, a difficult student is more than his or her problems.

So I answered the hall monitor's question with the following words: "I don't have problem students . . . just needing souls." I know he thought I was a bleeding-heart idiot.

ABOUT LABELS

We see many undesirable behaviors in our classrooms and we have names for almost all of them. These names were derived from teachers' assumptions about outward appearances. I say "assumptions" not "hypotheses" because the beliefs we usually have about student behavior have not been scientifically tested or even grounded in our own investigation. They are just what we think is going on. Looking beneath the surfaces of common inappropriate behaviors will not only help us to better understand them, but will also help us to know what we can do to change them.

Label: Lazy

Students who continually miss deadlines, do not turn in homework, or who slump in their seats and act disinterested are often thought to be lazy or, more politely, unmotivated. The dictionary definition of lazy is, "disliking . . . exertion" (Webster's Third Unabridged Dictionary, 1986, p. 1282). In my career, I have rarely met a student who dislikes exertion.[1] Students like to talk, run, bully, or argue, but most students are not guilty of disliking exertion. Listen to their taste in music: it is pounding with aggressive energy.

This raises a couple of questions. Why do students act lazy in our classrooms? Can a student be lazy about some things and not about others? And if so, how does that come about? To answer these questions about our students, let's first think about ourselves. Might we be energized about our subject area, say history, but lazy about cleaning the basement? Or excited about spring break, but lazy about grading finals? You see, everyone is lazy about some things. As a result, I prefer to use the term "reluctant" or "avoiding" to explain a person's lack of desire to accomplish something.

So, I believe, it is with students. Our students are "lazy" about their schoolwork for the same reason we are "lazy" about cleaning the basement. We anticipate being bored, feeling overwhelmed, getting frustrated, being cooped up inside, and experiencing unhappy feelings (giving away my children's baby clothes was pretty darn sad for me, and was one reason I delayed cleaning my basement). Students who struggle to learn, as well as those who are very advanced, anticipate few rewards from the hard—often boring—work ahead of them. For a kinesthetic learner, for example, sitting through a forty-five-minute (or these days a one-hundred-minute) lecture is not at all satisfying. For a mathematically gifted student, doing twenty-five problems at night when the first twenty were really easy seems like a waste of an inquisitive brain. For a young person whose hard work yields poor grades, schoolwork begins to seem worthless. Understand?

As far as I can tell, no one is born lazy. Babies are born highly curious and highly active. They have an innate drive to learn and they experience intrinsic joy when they do. They have to learn to suck, to recognize people, to use their hands, to crawl, to walk, to speak, to understand language, and to make sense of gravity, hot stoves, and crossing the street. Nature programs people with a strong desire to learn and to create. Human beings' primary self-defense capability is the creative intellect, after all we can out-smart predators and create the things we need to survive.

Then why are so many of our blue jay students lazy? Remember, I prefer to say "reluctant" and "avoiding", rather than "lazy". These students base their nonmotivation on an unconscious cost-benefit analysis. How much effort and risk of self-esteem are required compared to the probable benefit? If a student expects to spend most or all of his or her unstructured time studying in order to be rewarded with boredom or a paper full of red marks, then the cost of trying is not worth it. The pay-off, the success, is missing. If the cost includes giving up time on his or her more stimulating activities, such as repairing the engine of a car or drawing comic book characters, then the natural joy of learning is also being thwarted. Eventually, the student becomes reluctant to keep trying to achieve at school. After years (maybe only months) of sacrifice, frustration, and discouragement, the student makes the unconscious choice to "opt out" of the high costs of school-based learning in order to avoid the pain and frustration of working at a losing business.

When looked at from this more in-depth perspective, we can see that what we interpret as the character flaw laziness is really a much sadder state of affairs. Once we recognize the underlying self-protective behavior that manifests as laziness, we have some possible therapeutic responses.

One, we can adjust our presentation of material to styles that are more interactive and less passive, thereby physically invigorating our most "laid-back" students. For example, an economics teacher I know teaches concepts experientially. His students run a small business in which they apply economic theory and earn money that later goes toward college scholarships for their own classmates.

Two, we can adapt our content to include current, seemingly more relevant issues. When we talk about reasons for the Vietnam War, for instance, we can add a discussion about the decision-making process for entry into the second war with Iraq.

Three, we can make time in class to walk our students through their work. I believe that true teaching is not telling information, making assignments, and grading them. True teaching is walking through the learning process side by side with students. This way, we can intervene before critical mistakes are made, provide incremental instruction, and assure greater degrees of success for our students. This will require time, patience, and perhaps political activism to allow for more flexibility in the curriculum.

Four, we can offer repeated positive feedback to our most success-needy students. We can identify and reward small successes along the way, such as lining up math problems neatly or writing an effective topic sentence. By so doing, we are improving the students' cost-benefit ratios. We are showing that they can achieve and providing them with some joy as a reward for their efforts. In addition, we just may be resparking their intellectual curiosity, this time in a supportive atmosphere.

Label: Irresponsible

We all know these people. They can't find a thing, their desks look like landfills, they do their work at the last minute, and they are always late. Interestingly, none of these qualities appear in Webster's (1986) definition of irresponsibility. The dictionary defines irresponsibility as having neither the authority nor the mental capability to make a decision or to be held accountable for certain actions. The kind of irresponsibility we are talking about has little to do with the care and leadership of other people. We are talking about the kind of irresponsibility that often has to do with petty things like pieces of paper or a few minutes.

More than in many other societies, ours holds punctuality and tidiness in high esteem. We tend to expect from all people the same innate ability to organize time and things. We also see lack of order and tardiness as a character flaw. We believe that disorganized people are lazy (there's that word again) and that if they just cared more they could be as neat and punctual as we are!

I have learned that disorder, procrastination, and tardiness have to do with a lot more than lack of will or lack of character. People with certain cognitive styles are more adept at ordering things and time management than others are. Just as we all have different faces and different tastes in food, we also have different mental styles for dealing with organizational matters.

Being organized and on time is an intellectual gift. Disorganized people may have others gifts. Ever notice, for instance, how highly creative people seem "flaky" when it comes to keeping track of things and appointments? The absent-minded professor stereotype comes to mind. There is evidence that energy levels of the highly creative brain follow different sequences than those of less-creative brains (Martindale and Armstrong, 1974). The brains of creative people, it seems, often make use of low brain-energy levels to allow themselves to reach out in multiple directions for as much information as possible. They also delay closure of thought for as long as possible before making decisions about ideas. Artists appear "scatter-brained" because they actually are scattering their perceptions and thoughts while searching for new ideas. When creative people do finally seize on ideas, their energy levels soar. They are late beginning work on their creative project, but they have enough energy to get the job done quickly at the last minute. In contrast, less creative people have a stronger need to find closure, and therefore, their brains tend to stay at a middle, more consistent energy level for a shorter period of time. This allows them to make decisions more quickly and to deal with fewer ideas in a more logical and organized fashion. What appear more or less like procrastination and irresponsibility may instead be the different modulations of different brains.

It is important to understand, however, that creative thinkers are not disorganized thinkers. They are quite skilled at organizing their new thoughts into functional theories, art forms, and inventions. They just are not as adept at organizing external materials, such as the paperwork on their desks or in their notebooks.

Creative thinkers also tend to perceive time differently from more methodical thinkers. Time, in this culture, is a rigidly regular rhythm of increments that many people can estimate accurately in their minds. Such people thrive on schedules, become accustomed to the time pattern of their day, can plan their activities to accommodate that pattern, and work steadily on a task until its completion.

For creative thinkers, accurate perception of time is a more difficult process. When deeply engaged in the almost trancelike focus of creative thought, creative folks will lose their sense of time. They lose their appetites and the need to go to the bathroom, too. Much time can pass in what seems like a short period. Einstein theorized that time is relative: its rate exists only in comparison to the regular pace of normal activities of the day. For the creative thinker, however, the pace of the day can be highly irregular. Sometimes the clock seems to tick at a "normal" rate, sometimes (as when engaged in creative activity) it ticks much faster than expected. And during those deep creative "trances," a creative person may give up her or his awareness of time altogether. For an artist, time can be like a wild animal in its unpredictability and its tendency to creep up when she or he is unaware.

As it is very difficult to tame a wild animal, it is also very difficult for such a thinker to manage time. Being late to class or an appointment may be less an act of irresponsibility than an inadequate attempt to estimate and put into order the earlier tasks of the day. Yet at school, we tend to treat tardiness as a moral flaw or personal affront and respond to it with punishments rather than understanding and guidance.

I have had a lifelong problem with punctuality, for example. In my life it has been both because I am poor at estimating how much preparation and travel time I will need, but also because I am highly motivated to accomplish as much as possible each day. As a result, I fall into the "just one more thing" trap. "I know I should be leaving," I think, "but maybe I can edit one more paragraph, or unstack the dishwasher, or make that quick phone call I've been putting off." So for me, tardiness has been more about being a responsible person who is trying to get all her work done than about being an irresponsible person who cares little if she is on time.

Which brings me to another point: not only are the brains of some people less adept at organizing the things and time of their real-world lives, but their values are often less inclined in that direction, as well. These people simply do not see the significance of being a few minutes late nor of a messy environment. In a creative mind, cleaning one's desk and organizing one's notebook, for instance, may pale in importance when pitted against thoughts about developing a cure for cancer, building the first solar-powered car, or making one's own prom dress. It is often frustrating to devote limited mental resources and time to something as mundane as alphabetizing the papers in a notebook or remembering where one's homework is.

This is not to say that creative people should be exempted from the need to live a reasonably orderly life. After all, they have to get where they need to go and have the requisite items with them at the time they arrive. What it does suggest, however, is that as teachers we need to interpret our students' behaviors with more knowledge and sensitivity. A student who is regularly messy or tardy may be blowing off your class, or he or she may be trying hard with the less-skilled part of his or her brain that organizes things. Harsh judgments and consequences for small infractions can build frustration and resentment. Teaching organizational and time-management strategies can work wonders.

I am sometimes amazed at how simple ideas can be huge insights to students. "Keesha" was a senior who seemed very capable of taking care of herself. My class was her first one after a lengthy "senior lunch" period. Though she expressed good intentions to make it on time, she was always late. She explained that she went home every day and took a nap on the couch during her lunch period, then overslept. She didn't mean to, but somehow couldn't wake herself up on time. I suggested that she set the timer on the oven to awaken her. With wide eyes, Keesha said "Wow, what a good idea." She was rarely late to my class again.

The universe needs those gifted with brains that organize things and time easily. They will maintain the structure of our families, institutions, and societies. The universe also needs our thinkers who tolerate disorganization. Chaos can give birth to creativity, according to many experts, for creativity is the building of a new structure out of the scattered pieces of the old.

Therefore, it seems to me that we should approach issues of organization and punctuality as we would problems with reading. We can help students identify their cognitive weakness, find effective strategies for compensating, and be careful to avoid blows to their self-esteem. If we recognize time and order as a continuum of possibilities rather than a black-and-white quality of character, we can relax our own anxiety and need to punish. Instead we can spend our energies helping students to become more organizationally functional.

Label: Careless

I have worked with many teachers who characterized sloppy work with lots of mistakes as "careless." This label implies that a student did not care enough about her or his work to try hard. Yet I have seen young people care very much and work very hard, but still have messy and inaccurate papers.

While students, like all human beings, can be casual, cavalier, or haphazard about what they are doing, there are some more fundamental reasons why students' work may appear to be carelessly done. Motor, sensory, and cognitive challenges may be underlying messy work or work that skips details.

For instance, a young person who is thought to be careless because he or she colors outside the lines with scribbley strokes and forms his or her cursive letters sloppily may very well have weak fine-motor coordination. Dysgraphia is the term for a cognitive learning disability that affects handwriting. A student who does not form small letters or pictures correctly, read "the small print," copy accurately from a blackboard, and color or write neatly may have vision acuity difficulties or visual learning disabilities such as dyslexia.

Some children have learning styles (right hemisphere preferences, for example) that predispose them to seek global, "big picture" approaches to understanding information. Work that asks for highly detailed focus may be difficult and boring to such learners.

Motor or sensory difficulties and atypical cognitive styles often cause children to produce work that seems to be "careless." However, when identified, these challenges can be corrected or adapted to easily. We can recommend vision testing, use larger print, relax our perfectionism, encourage students to use a computer rather than handwriting for assignments, and plan our lessons to address multiple learning styles. As a result, our students will be able to show us that they are not so careless, after all.

Label: Just Trying to Get Attention

When her teacher wasn't looking, a high school girl drew a large penis on the wall with permanent marker. After she was caught, she showed no remorse for her action. The teacher called the girl's home, at which time the father asserted that he would take care of it. Having talked with a parent and earlier with the school discipline office, the teacher felt that she had done what was necessary. I asked if she found out why the girl had made the drawing. "Oh, she was just trying to get attention." I have no doubt that she was.

Throughout my career, I have heard teachers and guidance counselors dismiss inappropriate student behavior as insignificant attention-getting behavior. They sometimes turn up their noses as if the student is burdening them by trying to get attention. But rarely does anyone ask themselves the profound question, "Why does he or she need this attention?"

There are some possible answers to think about.

- As we discussed previously, all human beings have innate needs for attachment, to be cared about by someone. Children who are not having their emotional needs attended to at home will seek attention elsewhere.
- Many people feel invisible. Powerful people in their lives ignore them, interrupt them, and attend to other members of the family, class, or social group while neglecting them. Feeling invisible can be worse than feeling disliked because it calls into question the basic validation of one's existence. People who feel invisible may go to great lengths seeking acknowledgment, response, and a voice. When avenues for positive recognition are blocked, the other route is often one of disruption, confrontation, and sometimes violence. Via this route, a young person can, at least, feel that he or she is alive.
- A young person may have a serious problem that needs professional intervention, but which seems too embarrassing or too overwhelming to speak about outright. Getting attention is a way of getting someone else to "ask the right question."

In the case of the aforementioned graffiti artist, I have a hypothesis. In my experience it is not uncommon for adolescent boys who are "feeling their oats" and marveling at their newfound sexuality to make drawings of reproductive organs of both genders. However, it is quite rare for girls to make pictures of penises. The obvious sexual content of the drawing by the female student in our story suggests that there may be something sexually troubling going on in her life. Incest? Date rape? Promiscuity? Since the matter was not pursued, I do not know the answer. But I worry. If the girl was being sexually abused by her father, the very man who said, "I'll take care of this," then what are the consequences going to be for the girl? Even if the problem is not related to her father, what are the consequences of letting her underlying problem go unresolved?

Inappropriate attention-getting behavior is a potent indicator that a student has significant unmet needs. We can choose to ignore, demean, and/or punish the child. However, when we sit down with the child, discuss his or her motivations, and listen carefully for hints at bigger issues, then we will be adequately addressing the real problem at hand.

ONE MORE THING ABOUT LABELS

Whenever I am at a meeting with all the teachers of a particular student and his or her parents, I am very aware of the labels teachers use to describe the struggling student. My red flags go up when I hear a student consistently characterized as disorganized, lazy, and careless. Why? Because these can also be manifestations of learning disabilities.

My son lived with an undiagnosed learning disability until he was twenty years old. He was very bright as a preschooler, always interested in learning. By the end of kindergarten, he had received speech therapy for three different maladies. When he learned to put consonants on the beginnings and ends of his words, he began to lisp. Once he corrected his "tongue-thrust" problem, he started to stutter.

In first grade, he was put in the gifted program, where his creative writing was deemed imaginative and successful, especially since spelling and grammar were not requisites. In second grade his language-arts gifted services teacher began to complain that he disliked writing. Of course, this was the year that he was forced to write all his assignments in cursive. He struggled with cursive writing, held his pencil in an unusual manner, and felt that his ideas were stifled by the extreme effort it took for him to write them down. At the end of the year he was removed from the gifted class.

In fifth grade, a substitute teacher was so enraged by his disorganized desk, that she humiliated him by dumping it upside down in front of the class. In sixth grade, a teacher threw away his paper without grading it because he forgot to put his name on it. In ninth grade, when he was already taking Enriched Algebra II, his math teacher allowed students to laugh at him when his questions referred back to previously discussed information. In tenth grade, he spent half of his school days in a more self-directed, student-centered alternative program. As a senior, he refused to participate in graduation at his home school.

During his freshman year in college, a special education teacher in my school asked me why my son went to an expensive private college instead of the near-by state university. I explained that he had a "very unique learning style" and he chose a college that matched his cognitive needs. She then made an off-the-cuff statement that I will never forget. She said, "When an 'LD' (learning disabled) kid with a [superior] IQ is in a regular program, he'll get Bs and Cs and no one will know he has a problem." She had described Tony, exactly.

While it was hard to find someone who knew how to test a twenty-year-old for learning disabilities, we found a wonderful psychologist. It was discovered that Tony had a language learning disability, and we were also surprised to learn that he showed evidence of attention-deficit. His speech disorders, his illegible handwriting, his trouble organizing school materials, his apparent carelessness toward school papers, his out-of-sequence questions in Algebra class were all symptoms of hidden learning disabilities, not the character flaws and laziness for which he had been punished.

Now a college graduate, my son still has an obviously unique cognitive style, but he is also driven by his creativity to write music and novels. He reads Kafka for pleasure. He has an active life inside his brain, though communicating about it in spoken language is still not his cup of tea. He keeps his apartment organized, takes care of his business, and enjoys his life—despite a K–12 experience that should have cost him his self-esteem.

As teachers, we are entrusted with our students' delicate senses of self-worth. We have the power to nurture or extinguish their motivation to learn. Let us not, ourselves, be lazy, irresponsible, and careless in our assessments of these young learners. Let us approach our students' shortcomings with constant awareness of their dignity. Let us see symptoms rather than flaws. Instead of labels, let us offer them hope, help, and self-worth.

NOTE

1. An exception is severe depression. Teachers can be the first ones to recognize symptoms and recommend professional intervention.

7.1. The Rich Get Richer and the Poor Get Poorer *by Nicole Gnezda*

7

THE POOR GET POORER: WHY REWARDS AND PUNISHMENTS DO NOT WORK

Earl Oremus is a principal at Marburn Academy in Columbus, Ohio, a school for young people with learning disabilities. During a presentation to parents of children with Attention Deficit Hyperactivity Disorder (ADHD), he explained why conventional behavior-management strategies do not work well. ADHD students, he explained, have weak executive function capabilities in the frontal lobes of their brains. They do not have reliable impulse control, they act before they think, and they tend to base their responses on emotion rather than intellect information. Many of our blue jay students are students with ADHD. However, even students without ADHD may exhibit similar symptoms, though the precipitating causes may be different. As with ADHD, kids with chronic, unmet emotional needs may not rely on their intellects to control behaviors because their intellectual functions are superceded by their painful, emotional states of mind. When we educators impose artificial, unpleasant consequences (punishments) on "sensitized kids" (Oremus, 2004), we aggravate the already out-of-kilter balance between their intellects and emotions by contributing more hurt to their already shamed and pained psyches. Then, by publicly offering pleasant reenforcements to other students, we further remind our blue jays of their failures, inadequacies, and "badness," thereby further sensitizing their emotions.

Most of us have no idea that we are making things worse by using these conventional behaviorist methods because throughout our careers, we have been trained to accept some inaccurate beliefs about student behavior. These beliefs, many of which were presented by Earl Oremus, include

- Reasoning and rationality are the primary functions for all students.
- Behavior is volitional and students make good or bad choices.
- All students are equally capable of making good choices about behavior.
- Students perceive and understand the relationship between their actions and the resulting consequences.
- Painful consequences will produce insightful self-reflection about one's behavior and the motivation to make changes in the future.

Because of these inaccurate beliefs, we create our classroom and schoolwide discipline plans accordingly. We continue to reenforce what we perceive to be "good behaviors" with praise, awards, and tokens such as candy or stickers. "Bad" behaviors we reenforce with shame, criticism, failure, emotional pain, loss of empowerment, withdrawal of love, and sometimes—unfortunately—corporal punishment (further abuse).

Kids who come to school rich with love from home, years of success, and a healthy sense of their own worth are given more strokes, praise, and validation. Their histories of success foster more success. They get richer.

However, our blue jay students come to school with deficits of life skills, psyches in pain, and well-developed failure complexes. By negatively reenforcing their inappropriate behaviors, we withdraw more from their already depleted personal resources, and they end up with even less self-esteem, competence motivation, and strength to try again to succeed at school. In the process, we also neglect to give them what they need most: positive attention, information, help, a sense of personal value, and hope. Thus, blue jay students get poorer.

For a moment, let us consider the consequences of these behaviorist discipline strategies.

- Students' emotional problems get worse.
- Much of the undetected pain and frustration that students bear erupts into violence at school.
- Teacher anxiety and burnout increase because of the pervasiveness of disciplinary disruptions and threats on the job.
- High numbers of students drop out of school altogether.
- "Not getting caught" becomes a dominant ethic.
- Students, even successful ones, do not internalize information. They learn only enough to get desired grades and behave only well enough to avoid getting in trouble. They become good people-pleasers rather than inquisitive scholars and ethical people.
- Students lack intrinsic motivation. They are trained to work for a reward not for the internal satisfaction of meaningful accomplishment.
- Therefore, many young people feel empty because they have not developed senses of themselves as interesting, empowered, competent, contributing members of society nor have they experienced the joys of curiosity, knowledge pursuit, and personal accomplishment.
- Schools are contributing to the cultivation of a national mentality that honors the acquisition of things well above the pursuit of knowledge, creativity, and the value of working for the health and welfare of other human beings.

By basing our schools and classrooms on behaviorist philosophy, we teachers may inadvertently be creating (or at least exacerbating) the very problems we believe we are correcting. What a shame. Our intentions are, without question, to help the young people in our care. It's too bad that we have been misled about how to do it.

Behaviorist discipline strategies have even wider sociological consequences, as well. They help to create a caste system in our schools. It is a caste system based on compliance to rules, and it relegates to the lowest rung those kids who come to school with the most severe personal challenges.

This school caste system shows up not just within an individual school population, but also across the range of schools in our country. Children from lower socioeconomic backgrounds tend to be less successful in school, to be more likely to drop out before completing high school, and to exhibit more blatant aggressive behaviors. Family income is not the deciding factor, however. A variety of other resources can be limited for families from the lower echelons of society. Such families are more likely to be parented by one adult, often a busier and more stressed parent, at that. Families with fewer financial resources have less access to affordable health care for mental health and substance abuse issues as well as education about parenting, crisis management, and child development. Children of lower socioeconomic status are more likely to have parents who are poorly educated, as well. These parents may not only be unable to help with schoolwork but also may bring their own anxieties, resentments, and histories of school failure to their relationships with their children. Families from marginalized ethnic groups have even more challenges to meet. Language barriers, differing customs and values, discrimination, and multigenerational histories of poverty or violence contribute to the burden for children trying to assimilate into a mainstream school culture.

It is common knowledge that schools in lower socioeconomic areas have lower achievement and lower test scores than those in the more privileged upper-middle-class suburbs. Unfortunately, the prevailing national attitude is often a behavioristic one, as well: Blame teachers for the lack of student achievement in the most economically and socially deprived areas of the country, then penalize the schools in which they teach. Thus, national policy is contributing to the educational caste system and blaming educators for it at the same time. Our national and state governments should, instead, be providing additional resources so schools can implement interventions to help their needy students overcome their enormous social and emotional obstacles to school success. Even schools in upper-income neighborhoods need to consider the advantages of implementing nonbehavioristic discipline strategies and mental health interventions within their facilities.

I clearly remember my father's frequent chant from his bed by the television when he felt compelled to complain about politics: "The rich get richer and the poor get poorer!" So it is with conventional behaviorist systems of discipline. Those young people who are fortunate enough to be free of academic handicaps, raised to understand the schema of civil social interaction, have belief in their own value and dignity, and who have learned to be self-regulating human beings are offered daily rewards and affirmations. They get the good grades, academic honors, varsity letters, citizenship awards, and smiley faces and stickers on their papers. They are the "rich" ones at school. However, those who live lives complicated by social, family, mental health, cognitive, and emotional issues are on the receiving end of punishments, verbal put-downs, and low grades. They are the poor. And they tend to get poorer—emotionally, academically, and eventually socioeconomically.

8.1. Pencil Drawing *by Sherman Hall, Student*

8

WE WON'T BE WIMPS!

I once had a friendly argument with a colleague who was also a high school football coach. I am a size four petite, he is the size of a grizzly bear. His taunting assertion was that I could never be competent to coach a football team. He based his argument not on my knowledge of the game (about which I admitted needing remedial work) but on my size and gender. He could not imagine me being able to keep these boys in line, because he believed I could have no effective influence over them. He thought it takes a big man to teach big boys. I was sure he was wrong.

The coach had failed to realize that I had already taught dozens of his players every day in my classes. He had also failed to realize that there are many effective ways to exert influence over students without having to be bigger, stronger, and scarier than they are. Being a successful leader in the classroom is not about raw, physical power or even swift and severe punishments. It is really about clarity of thought, the courage to nurture, and relationship building.

CLARITY OF THOUGHT

For us to be teachers who facilitate student growth in our classrooms instead of the entropy of apathy and aggression, we first need to clarify our thoughts about student behavior, that is, to examine our expectations, requirements, and boundaries.

I resist using the term "rules," because I believe that rules has pejorative connotations. Just as a measuring-stick ruler is unchanging and hard-edged, its related word "rules" implies authoritarianism, rigidity, and focus on negative behaviors. The term "expectations," however, anticipates positive behavior, "requirements" implies a needed contribution from students, and "boundaries" suggests clear limitations.

As effective leaders, we need to determine expectations, requirements, and boundaries that will make everyone comfortable in our classrooms. The limits we set up for our classrooms should have two primary goals: to protect the physical and psychological safety of every person in the classroom and to promote an atmosphere that facilitates learning. Meeting our personal tastes or satisfying our psychological needs for control, authority, and power are generally counterproductive and are our own business to work out. Our focus should always be on creating an atmosphere that maximizes learning for all the students.

To identify the expectations, requirements, and boundaries that we each need in our own, unique classrooms, we should consider the following questions and write down the answers.

- What do I value?
  For instance, human dignity, individuality, work ethic, and creativity may be some of the values we choose.
- What are the boundaries needed to prevent hurtful and/or nonproductive activities from occurring in the classroom?
  Keep in mind that psychological safety is as important a prerequisite of learning as physical safety is.
- How do I organize learning activities? Where is room for deviation in my plan? How might I adapt my planned activities for deviation?
  Homework is an example. Suppose a teacher has given twenty-five math problems a night for homework throughout his whole career.

He answers student questions the next day, grades the homework in class, and then moves on. That is his organization plan. However, there is room for flexibility and there are reasons he might have for deviating from his plan, such as eliminating busywork, changing the quantity and the quality of the work, and achieving the primary goal, which is learning. He could give a proficiency quiz at the end of his presentation to determine who does and does not need homework to help them understand the new concepts. He could reduce the number of problems and expect students to spend more homework time examining the processes they are learning. He could set up homework teams to do homework together to ensure that everyone understands the concepts.

As we study our own organization plans, we should look for the underlying goals of each aspect and then examine if our plans are really meeting our educational goals.

- What are all the student needs I can think of? How might I be able to accommodate them?.

  Examples might be: the need to be heard when they contribute to a discussion, to talk with us privately when something is happening in their lives, for one-on-one help, to be alone when they feel overstimulated, to eat when their blood sugar is dropping, and to talk to friends during class. I will decide which ones I can accommodate, based on the values listed in the first question, and which ones seem frivolous.

- What are my idiosyncratic needs?

  For example, when I speak I need to be heard. I have an issue with feeling invisible and am, therefore, not comfortable when talking to a class if students are turned away from me, sleeping, doing homework, or having their own conversations. Other teachers may need to make eye contact with students or may just hate whining. Whatever special needs we have, they count. What don't count are our wants. I want all students to dress according to my standards. I want my students to always speak without their cultural dialects. I want students to organize their notebooks according to my system. I want to stand by the door and catch anyone who is even a second late to my class.

Now, prioritize the lists of values and needs and choose only the most important ones. This is an important step. A few significant and well-grounded rules are much more effective than long lists of picky ones. Too many rules are hard to manage and, what is more, the really important ones will lose their potency when grouped with lots of trivial ones.

No one can have everything he or she wants, so we adults have to decide what the most important boundaries and expectations are going to be. Some are non-negotiable. That everyone should be free to ask questions without ridicule is non-negotiable, for instance. Some rules serve only to make us teachers more comfortable and have little educational rationale. Examples are statements like "I won't accept papers without names," "no water bottles in the classroom no matter how thirsty your medication may make you," or "late work is never accepted." Decide that student learning is the highest goal, and pleasing our tastes and making our jobs easier is not.

Once we have clarified our thinking about our expectations, requirements, and boundaries, the next step is to find the courage to enforce them. Remember that courage comes from the heart, not just from exerting our power with brute force.

THE COURAGE TO NURTURE

The obvious courageous act is to enforce our boundaries. The more important courageous act is to enforce them compassionately. Since the purpose of enforcing our expectations is to get compliance, we need to respond to students in ways that will truly gain compliance, not just for the present moment but for the long term. Ideally, we want students, even our difficult students, to internalize our lessons about behavior and become better functioning people. To make this growth happen, we must nurture the student at the same time we enforce our boundaries.

Nurturing our students requires us to consider options for response that exclude punishments and rewards. Yes, systems of punishment and reward are based on "coercion" (Glasser, 1992) and "bribes" (Kohn, 1993), were championed by a man who believed that "total control of a living organism" was a "fascinating thing" (B. F. Skinner, cited in Kohn, 1993, p. 19), and are antithetical to real, intrinsic growth.

It may seem scary to consider eliminating the standardized consequences (punishments) inherent in traditional classroom discipline because we fear we may lose control of our classes. We tend to rely on
punishments for three reasons: we assume they work, we can handle disciplinary matters quickly without much emotional engagement, and we
feel gratified that we "got" or "nailed" (in actuality, got back at) the one
who disrupted our leadership, irritated us, and violated our rules. Yet
these methods often do not work for our blue jay students. Externally
imposed consequences are not deterrents for difficult students' unacceptable behavior because, as previously discussed, most difficult students either do not intrinsically understand the modus operandi of their
schools or may view the punishments as more fuel for their resentment,
rebellion, and apathy. It might seem less scary to think about abandoning
our old, reliable, behaviorist methods if we begin to realize that they may
be causing more problem behaviors than they are preventing.

Dealing with problem behaviors in private, nurturing ways can be
much more effective than the overt "power-plays" of a classic behaviorist approach. Carefully chosen words can make positive change seem
desirable to students. Being treated with respect for their dignity and
self-esteem can encourage blue jay students to listen to what we have to
say and to grow in self-discipline, instead of reverting to their usual dysfunctional, self-protective behaviors, the ones that caused problems in
the first place.

But how do we discipline in this nurturing way?

Start with the simplest, least emotionally charged response.

- "No," "not in school," or nonverbal signals act as nonthreatening re-
  minders of our expectations.
- Redirecting student behavior is often effective: offer another activity, place to sit, or use for a utensil. If students resist, as they in-
  evitably do, then we need to stand our ground until they comply,
  remove the offending item from their hands, or take them gently
  by the arm and walk them to a new seat.
- We can try to ignore further attention-getting behavior. It's a hard
  call to know when to respond to a student and when to pretend to
  be engaged in another activity. Ignoring only works if a student
  knows that you are ignoring him or her as a negative response to his

or her behavior (Newman and Newman, 1978, p. 325). Use this strategy to avoid an argument or power-struggle or as a means to signal to a student, "talk is over, time to get to work."

• Proximity is often a very effective means for nonverbally stopping undesirable student behaviors. Walking across the room in the middle of a lecture and positioning oneself right next to a noisy or disengaged student gets her or his attention and makes it uncomfortable for that student to continue her or his inappropriate behaviors. Sometimes a teacher can sit down next to a student or group of students while they work, either becoming directly involved in their learning process or at least doing the teacher's own work right in the midst of the student's territory.

Most of these simple and/or subtle strategies are not news to an experienced teacher. But sometimes we forget to try them and, instead, bring out the big guns too soon.

For more serious or intractable behaviors, the following in-depth strategies are often effective.

1. Avoid power-struggles. Blue jay students will try to get us into a power-struggle because it is their normal means of dealing with conflict and because it triggers a satisfying adrenaline rush. If possible, walk away from a student long enough to gain composure. Set aside a more appropriate time when the issue can be addressed in a calm manner. This can easily occur when the other students are engaged in independent work, such as during a study period at the end of class.

2. If necessary, impose a time-out on the student. Remove him or her to the hall or an isolated seat. Explain that this is not punishment but a way of removing the disruptions from the class and giving the student a chance to calm his or her emotions. This will maintain a respect for the student's dignity while putting an end to the undesirable behavior. Time alone, outside of the classroom or the view of his or her peers, will provide an opportunity to disempower the emotions and quell the adrenaline rush.

3. Begin to think of the problem not as a "the student against me" but as a learning challenge that student and teacher will pursue to-

gether. That means that we teachers have to overcome our own anger before we interact with the student.

4. When the time and location are right, begin a calm, fair, and intellectual discussion with the student about the offending behavior and need for change. Speak in loving tones, if possible, or at least in emotionally honest but controlled tones. During the discussion, follow The Seven-Step Plan for Positive Discipline, figure 8.1.

At this point in our discussion, I am sure that we are all feeling overwhelmed by the thought of spending this much time on one student's behavior. Yet we would not hesitate to spend extra time reexplaining a math concept, editing a paper, or otherwise tutoring a student who needs a little more instruction. Why should we react differently when the need is instruction in how to behave? Somehow we find time for conferences with students *about course content* and conferences with parents *about students' behavior*. We can find time for conferences *with students*, as well. Sometimes a few conferences with students about how and why they should behave will eliminate the need to spend time in parent conferences and tutoring sessions down the road.

This nurturing approach will require of us some things besides time. It will require patience, because change is slow, just as learning any other major concept is often slow. It will require that we commit ourselves to trying this new approach over the long term, helping the student grow incrementally toward self-discipline. Herman (1997, p. 148) cautions clinical therapists to expect "repeated testing, disruption, and rebuilding of the relationship," advice that pertains to teachers, as well. A nurturing approach will require that we get engaged with the student in the creative process of problem solving. It will also require us to have the courage to abandon comfortable old methods that are ineffective. But it will be worth it.

Nurturing via a problem-solving approach to enforcing our classroom boundaries will work. It will work because we will use tones of voice, word choices, strategies, and real consequences that reenforce students' human dignity. All the while, we will also be changing the mental constructs, belief systems, and needs-gratification devices that have previously guided their behaviors. It will work because we will be building

SEVEN-STEP PLAN FOR POSITIVE DISCIPLINE

1. *Identify in specific terms the inappropriate behavior.* Honestly, some kids do not know that certain behaviors are problematic.
2. *Explain reasons behind rules (i.e., to educate).* Reasons might include interfering with other people's needs, hurting other people's feelings, interfering with our own needs and feelings, ethical considerations, what is good for society as a whole, and helping the student to meet his or her own future needs and goals.
3. *Listen to the student's feelings.* This is an important step because it will give you the information necessary to formulate a future disciplinary response. Require that the student express himself or herself with respectful tones and words, if necessary. The student's presentation may be very passionate or energized because he or she needs time to vent his or her emotions.
4. *Apologize for anything you did that was unfair or hurtful,* such as losing control of emotions, saying demeaning things to the student, using an insulting tone of voice, or violating the student's rights or dignity. This may be difficult for some teachers because we fear that we will be compromising our power. On the contrary, we will be gaining power by communicating to our students that we also have high expectations for our own behavior and that we only want to do what is right and beneficial for the student. In this way we will be building trust, a very significant motivator of students.
5. *Point out the natural or real consequences of the student's behavior,* rather than imposing artificial, punitive consequences. Blue jay students seem to have very little recognition of the relationship between their actions and subsequent incidents. Illuminate for them the effects of their actions on the people around them. Explain to them how their current actions will naturally trigger other, often unpleasant, events in their own lives. And show how reckless behaviors can precipitate a series of events that result in very serious problems down the road.
6. *Problem solve.* Discuss possible fair resolutions to the disciplinary problem. Solicit suggestions from the student of what she or he might do to atone for the offense. The student will undoubtedly have trouble coming up with ideas, as she or he has been well trained to be punished and/or avoid being punished. Help the student think creatively. Switch roles and ask what she or he would want if she or he were the teacher. Possible resolutions include: a written apology to the injured party; replacement of damaged items; completing a task similar to the one a student omitted (cleaning out a cupboard to make up for leaving a mess in classroom); and a soul-searching creative work that helps the student come to terms with her or his behavior. Example of the latter was asked of a high school art student when she had cut class. Instead of assigning a detention, the teacher asked the student to keep a journal of thoughts about why she had cut class. This turned out to be a much more difficult task than the normal punitive "consequence." In the end, the student created a highly emotive painting about the feelings that were involved during and after the commission of her offense.
7. *Seek to ameliorate the situation.* Identify strategies for avoiding misbehavior in the future. Anything from changing one's seat to finding a study buddy, to asking to take a break, to getting counseling can be on the table for discussion.

positive, functional relationships with young people whose histories have included far too few examples of them.

RELATIONSHIP BUILDING

As a result of nurturing, growth-oriented interactions with difficult students, we may obtain significant information about the underlying causes of their behaviors. This is important information because the real solution to disruptive and aggressive behaviors is to solve the problems that underlie them. We can begin to do this only after we have developed a trusting, meaningful relationship with a student.

Once students begin to trust us to care about them as human beings and not just little learning machines, then they begin to reveal their true needs. We get to find out what is really going on. For instance, maybe a student's homework is rarely done because he or she doesn't understand it and feels too stupid to turn in a paper that will be a failure. Or because his or her father drinks and becomes abusive at night. Or because his or her after-school hours are occupied babysitting younger siblings while their single mother works the night shift. We begin to see that missing homework assignments are but a symptom. Now we can address the real problems that are underlying the student's behavior.

When I ask students "Are you okay?" I am surprised at how willing they are to tell me really personal information about their life struggles and pain. They express themselves with force, as they expel feelings that have been tightly bottled up for a long time. I watch their pained faces turn from screwed up and sour to relieved, as small smiles grow across their busily talking mouths. Young people are usually quite eager for help with their perplexing personal problems. Revealing them to a trusted adult is a first step in the process of changing their lives.

Change is slow and happens from the inside out. At first, we may not see it at all. A colleague and I have had many talks about our frustrations that students do not change as much or as rapidly as we would like. We have decided that what sometimes seems to us like work in vain is really sowing. The seeds we plant in our classrooms now may take root later, when our students mature or have control over their own lives. In the future our seeds may precipitate true personal renaissances in their futures.

And if not? Even if our students' lives never get better, even if they spiral downward and end up in terrible trouble or pain, our work with them will not have been in vain because we will not have contributed to the downfall. Instead, we will have truly connected with the student, even though it was for a short time in her or his life. For a while, the student was not alone, the student was not anonymous or invisible, the student was not insignificant. As teachers, we will have at least tried to help a young person change her or his life by building an authentic, honest, and human relationship.

WIMPS

Contrary to common misbelief, teachers who forego punitive discipline strategies and rely, instead, on clarity of thought, nurturing, and positive relationships are not wimps in their classrooms. Teacher-wimps are, instead, of two main varieties: those who let their students run amok in class and those who blindly follow a preestablished set of rules and regularly send students to someone else (e.g., the principal, the dean, etc.) to be "disciplined."

The former are afraid to assert themselves, to hear themselves speak forcefully and with passion, and be the bad guy. Or maybe they are small, gentle people who try hard to be authoritarian and fail because it is against their nature.

The latter are like the old-fashioned mother who would tell her children, "Just wait until your father gets home to punish you." She would not claim the strength, feel the emotions, or do the work necessary to discipline her children herself. Teachers like this, who regularly pass on disciplinary tasks to others in the school, are acting much like their difficult students: opting out instead of getting involved.

However, caring teachers who humanely enforce clear expectations create an irresistible strength in the classroom. The authenticity of their purpose and compassion for the situations of their students lay the groundwork for mutual respect. They take the initiative to establish limits and have the courage to get into the raucous and maybe get dirty—

to, whenever possible, address classroom behaviors all by themselves. They also seek understanding of how to resolve the underlying problems that caused the ruckus to occur in the first place. When we discipline in this way, we, too, will be steadfast and wise leaders in our students' young lives and effect real changes in their behavior. We will model for them and expect from them the highest qualities of human character: wisdom, courage, and compassion.

The result of this humane approach is much more than gaining short-term compliance to our expectations. In fact, it is no less than influencing the character development of our students.

9.1. Coeurage *by Nicole Gnezda*

9

MORE ABOUT COURAGE

It takes courage to be a compassionate teacher to our blue jays. If we listen to their authentic thoughts and feelings, we might be told things that we don't want to know. They might tell us about their suicidal thoughts or their alcoholic parents. What do we do then? We are not psychologists and may not know what to do next. We might not want to break our denial that such things happen. We also might not want to get involved.

It takes courage to be a compassionate teacher to our blue jays because we might have to face ourselves and do some growing, too. It is hard to hear from a student that something we are doing in the classroom is not working for him or her. It hurts and is abrasive to our own feelings of inadequacy.

It takes courage to adapt our teaching styles and to try something new. Creative growth is always a scary thing. It threatens us with chaos. It asks us to step in a new direction without having a mental picture of where the trip will take us.

"Courage" is related to the French word "coeur," meaning "heart." Courage means "having heart," enough heart to accomplish the frightening and difficult. In his book *The Courage to Create* (1975), psychologist Rollo May discussed four types of courage: perceptual, moral, social, and creative. Perceptual courage is the willingness to let oneself sense the suffering of others. Becoming aware of someone's pain requires courage because it will undoubtedly make us hurt, too.

Moral courage is the strength to do what is right on behalf of other human beings. It takes courage to do what is morally right because it may very well get us into trouble with our peers and superiors.

Social courage is the ability to risk oneself in order to have meaningful relationships with others. According to May, the essential need of human life is attachment, to love and be loved. However, when a person seeking love opens up to someone else, he or she also risks rejection—hence the need for social courage.

Creative courage is the fortitude to look beyond what is comfortable and to envision new possibilities. In order to create a new way of teaching, or disciplining, or living, we must be able to endure the disorder that comes with change. Things will fall apart so that we can see the pieces and put them into a new, more functional, more elegant order. Creativity is how we sense problems and find real solutions. It is hard work. It is the opposite of entropy. It is what makes life in this universe keep on going.

How important is it for us to courageously form caring, healing relationships with our difficult students and change our teaching styles accordingly? May believed that "the need for creative courage is in direct proportion to the degree of change a profession [and, I would add, a student body] is undergoing" (1975, p. 13). In the twenty-first century, change is the only thing we can depend on. Therefore, creative courage as well as perceptual, moral, and social courage are of the utmost importance.

Teachers have courage. We know we would run back into our burning schools to save one of our students or throw our bodies over our children to protect them from a tornado. Just going into school to teach every morning is sure evidence that we teachers are courageous people.

Though we should also be courageous with regards to our students' psychological needs, it is really scary to delve deeply into relationships with difficult kids. We might be wrong about how to help the students, say the wrong things, or make the problems worse. We might lose control of our own feelings or be overwhelmed by them. We might reveal more about ourselves than we are comfortable revealing. The situation might get out of our control. As a result, many of us act as if we are apathetic toward the needs of our students not because we are callous, unfeeling adults, but because we are afraid to become responsible for something at which we might fail. However, the stakes are high. We are talking about saving someone's spirit, or someone's life.

This is where courage comes in. All we need is the courage to try. If we listen to kids, we learn what is causing their suffering, that is, the motivation behind their difficult behaviors. Once we learn, we can seek answers. We can go to resource people such as counselors, interventionists, and school psychologists. We can find books, articles, or websites, and read, read, read. We can listen to radio and TV shows that teach about life issues. We can take graduate courses.

We do not have to have all the answers: we can teach young people how to find them. We do not have to say all the right things: we can listen in all the right ways. Most of all, we can build attachments with young people in need and model for them what caring is all about.

May said that a relationship is "like a chemical mixture, if one of us is changed, both of us will be. . . . [We] will not come out unaffected" (1975, p. 8). This is the good news. For, as our students begin to grow through their difficulties with us by their sides, we grow too. The depth of our characters, the fullness of our hearts, the wealth of our experiences all increase within us. We become bigger and better people as we help our students to see the possibilities for their own futures.

10.1. Pencil Drawing *by G. Anthony Smith, Age 3*

⑩

KEEPING IT SIMPLE

The most difficult course I encountered in graduate school was a qualitative research class taught by a forceful, fabulously intelligent woman with spiked hair. It was there that I first heard about the KISS Rule, which she said meant, "Keep it simple, Stupid." Of course, when I use the KISS Rule in my classroom, I prefer to say, "Keep it simple, Student." It is now time to apply the KISS Rule to our discussion of blue jay students.

Up to now, this book has taken us on a circuitous route through cognitive, affective, and aesthetic regions, a trip that may have left our heads very full. To help clarify our thinking, I have reduced the prior discussion down to the ten objectives listed in figure 10.1. They are meant not as expectations for perfection but directions toward which we can grow.

By striving toward these goals one step, one young person, one incident at a time, we will make incremental changes in ourselves and our students. We will interact with students in ways that are more likely to foster real improvement in their behavior. We will help break the chains of disruptive behaviors that come from unmet needs for self-protection, empowerment, and love. We will contribute to growth in the world and minimize the entropy in the lives of our students and our schools.

TEN OBJECTIVES FOR EFFECTIVE COMPASSIONATE DISCIPLINE

1. To be aware and sensitive to young people's basic psychological needs.
2. To define problem behaviors as dysfunctional attempts at needs gratification.
3. To be educated about psychology and counseling techniques, either through coursework or self-directed research.
4. To resolve our own psychological issues so that we do not act out our self-protective and empowerment needs on students.
5. To hesitate to rely on the standard "knee-jerk reactions" of scolding, shaming, punishing, and other behavior-modification strategies.
6. To be positive and creative. Problem solve situations, consider many possible responses before choosing one, and help students think up acceptable strategies that will more effectively get their needs met.
7. To be compassionate listeners by focusing on students' emotional pain rather than our own frustration and anger.
8. To be open to new approaches and to try them many times before passing judgment on their effectiveness.
9. To advocate in the school by educating our colleagues and working to implement new programs that will address students' underlying issues.
10. To use our expertise to advocate at the district, state, and national levels; to work for changes in the policies that interfere with effective teaching (such as high-stakes testing, large class sizes, zero-tolerance philosophies, and inadequate funding); to be vocal in our commitment to quality classrooms for our students and ourselves.

We adults expect our students to work steadily, even plug along, as they take incremental steps along the paths of knowledge and self-improvement. We advise them against giving up, even when the going gets tough. We tell them that they will eventually succeed.

As teachers who are learning a new vision of our difficult students and new approaches to working with them, we need to follow our own advice. There will be no magic changes in our students–or ourselves. But there will be a slowly developing improvement in the quality of our classroom relationships and the attitudes of our kids. There will be more smiling, even laughing, less blaming and backlash. As we see the lights begin to turn back on in the eyes of our blue jay students, we will notice that they are more engaged, maybe a little bit enthusiastic about learning. Our growing competence will be motivating to us, and we will become more and more effective teachers for all our students.

So let's not give up. We will take small steps and remember that our Ten Objectives for Effective Compassionate Teaching are not rigid rules. No, they are "truths worth laboring for" (Spitzmueller and James, 2002) because all of our students, even our blue jays, are worth our labor.

11.1. Overworked *by Nicole Gnezda*

⏸ WHY BOTHER?

That's a good question. Teaching is a really hard job, despite the common myth that we only work from eight to three and play all summer. We are exhausted at the end of each day. There is a never-ending list of things we still need to do. Why should we, then, work even harder than we already do? Why should we add to our to-do lists more things to learn? Why should we bother to try new strategies to reach our most challenging students?

BECAUSE OF CAROL

"Carol" was a petite, quiet, and creative teenager. She looked a little ragged, asked few questions, and made her class projects satisfactorily but without elaboration or enthusiasm. Her art, however, was personal and expressive.

When Carol was in my beginning drawing class, I assigned a self-portrait: "Not one that looks like you, but one that tells me who you are or how you see the world." My objectives were to provoke higher-level thinking, to teach about abstract art, and to encourage a high level of creativity. Carol set to work. Her imagery was simple but emotionally profound. Her self-portrait was a dark-blue person splayed out, crucifixion style. From the wounds in the hands and feet dripped the words "loneliness," "fear,"

11.2. Self-Portrait *by Anonymous Student Artist*

"hate," and "insecurity." The blue figure was posed in front of an all-black background.

Knowing it was a hard time in her life because of recent deaths in her family, I interpreted Carol's picture to be an expression of the grief she was experiencing. Soon, school was adjourned for summer vacation and, other than grading it, I did not follow up on Carol's drawing.

Carol was not in any of my classes the next year, though I saw her frequently. Every day, she ate her lunch alone, crouched in a space behind the art room's heavy door. I thought perhaps she liked the peace and quiet but also recognized that she might have been depressed. (It seems obvious now, but in the midst of the activity of a normal day at school, I barely noticed her.) One day I encountered her guidance counselor at our mailboxes and mentioned to her that I believed Carol needed some help for possible depression. The counselor gave me a somewhat puzzled look then remarked, as if I'd told her Carol was in the circus, "I think maybe she was on antidepressants last year." Since I had made this referral to Carol's counselor and since she wasn't even my student anymore, I thought my responsibilities were over.

During her junior year, Carol took another of my classes and then the next year came to me and asked if I still had one of the works of art she had left behind. I had lost it long ago, but to cover up my embarrassment, I said I would look for it. Later, feeling bad for not taking better care of her work, I told her simply that I couldn't find it.

School ended for the summer, and with a sigh of relief I left my students to their own lives and went home. It was only a couple of weeks later, after Carol had graduated, that her boyfriend was killed in a car accident. After Carol found out, she agonized for three weeks, then hung herself.

Carol's family asked that I not portray her as morose or oppositional, and, indeed she was neither. On the contrary, she was sweet, artistic, and kind. She and family made valiant attempts to deal with her depression off and on over the years. Perhaps her suicide was inevitable, but I still wonder. Carol's cries for help were expressed in the whispers of her mouse-sized body and mouselike countenance. Someone needed to roar for her, to watch over her at school, to make sure she was OK. It could have been me.

BECAUSE OF LEROY

"Leroy" was a young man who had been placed by juvenile court in a local group home for abused and delinquent children. As he was high school age and well behaved, he attended my late husband, Gary's, school and ran on his track team. Leroy was enthusiastic about his life, expressing a desire to better himself, to find his way in the confusing world outside of institutional life. He turned eighteen before graduation and was given special permission to continue living at the "Children's Home" and do odd jobs until he completed high school. He spent hours at our house, as Gary counseled him about his future life choices.

Leroy was interested in the local community college but finally decided to join the Army. When on leave he stayed with us, proudly showing off his Army photo. When he was discharged, he moved in with us for a couple of weeks. He played with our children and spent Christmas with us.

He was very unsure about what to do with his life. He thought again about college or about reenlisting in the service. Gary admonished him that, whatever he chose, he should never go back to his parents' home again. This is harsh advice, but Leroy had told us stories about his father doing unspeakable sexual and abusive acts. Leroy reenlisted, but was soon dishonorably discharged. With no guidance from the Army and no institutions to structure his life, he went home to his dad.

Within a few months, rumors were going around the school that someone with the same name as Gary's former student had been arrested for murder. At first we didn't believe it, but before long Leroy was on the phone. According to him, his father, brother, and he had picked up an underage girl, had sex with her (for which he was charged with rape), and his father had killed her with a screwdriver. Leroy swore that he had not helped kill her. He even refused a plea bargain in which he would have had to plead guilty in court to a crime he says he did not commit. As it turned out, his father was the prosecution's star witness!

Gary talked with Leroy on the phone from time to time, listening to his story and reenforcing his attorney's advice. For the last fifteen years, Leroy has been in prison. He may be there for the rest of his life.

My late husband had little power over the enormous events of Leroy's life. He could not neutralize the terrible influence of his father. He could not cleanse him of the dysfunction in his family. He could not make him intellectually and emotionally capable of what he was unable to do. But he could care about him.

Looking back on what I know of Leroy's life, I believe the months that Gary was his teacher and advisor were the only times Leroy was ever loved. As a teacher, Gary—and through him our family—offered Leroy the gift of self-worth. We encouraged him, believed in his value as a human being, and made him feel welcome. We gave him a glimpse of a stable and flourishing family life. We could not save him, but we could care about him. My children and I remember him. We have compassion for his circumstances and frailties. We speak of him from time to time and continue to wish him well.

Whenever I stop to think about Leroy, I also think of what he would have missed in his life if Gary had treated him only as "a dysfunctional kid from the children's home" instead of as a person of significance.

BECAUSE OF ALEXIS

"Alexis" was a beautiful, artistic student. She sat in the back of the room and worked diligently on her projects. Intuitively, I felt her to be a person of warmth and character. I thought she was popular and problem free.

When she was developing an idea for her self-portrait, she began to reveal some personal problems. Her feelings were fragile and her sense of self weak. On a later project, she asked to speak privately with me and told of a difficult struggle with anorexia. I listened closely to stories about her parents' liberal spending of money and extreme stinginess with love and affirmation. In Alexis's eyes, her parents were domineering and demeaning. I was shocked to hear that, despite her father's knowledge of her eating disorder, he would tap her tummy and make fun of the little bulge that was there. She reported that she felt ugly, because her parents were unwilling to acknowledge any beauty in her appearance. She felt like a failure because her parents did not praise any of her achievements. They did not even recognize any of the person that Alexis was inside, which made her feel invisible to the most significant people in her life.

Because Alexis was in counseling and because her figure still appeared rather full, I chose to keep our interaction private, and to monitor her and talk with her whenever she wanted. We spent many minutes in the hall while her classmates worked on their art. Beautiful Alexis continued to tell me about feeling worthless, unattractive, and invisible to her parents. Her only role in life was to be successful at academics and sports and to receive her parents' expensive gifts.

I hugged her and shared my very different opinion of her. I told her that she was beautiful and valuable to the world. I helped her see how her anorexia was an insidious way of proving her parents right by making herself slowly disappear. We talked about issues of control. I tried to supplement her professional treatment program with my own love and support.

The next year, Alexis was again in my class. She told me that she was no longer anorexic—the clinic program had worked. But now she was bulimic. Again I assessed her body mass. Fearing that involving her parents would exacerbate her anguish, I encouraged her back to the clinic. While she continued seeing the therapist at the clinic, she and I talked. I was a nonjudgmental ear to whom she could vent. I was someone who knew her (through her artwork as much as our conversations). I was someone whose belief in her value could help neutralize the attacks by her parents.

During Thanksgiving vacation, I was quite worried about Alexis, since the holiday is laden with both family and food. We talked as soon as possible after school resumed. She seemed like a different person. No, the food wasn't a problem. And, yes, something special had happened. She had visited cousins over vacation, and they found her fascinating. She was the center of their attention because of her ability to draw. As she related her story, her speech was full of energy, her face a rainbow of expressions. She talked so much I could hardly keep up with her.

She also told me of a breakthrough that had occurred to her during therapy. She had learned from me that she no longer had to believe the negative assessments dumped on her by her parents, but until now, she did not know what to replace them with. Her therapist had suggested a workout program as a substitute for the no-food strategy with which she had been obsessed, and he taught her to fill her emptiness with her own interests. Alexis was finally alive.

She has since grown from making honest but ugly paintings that acknowledge her pain and mistreatment to bright, free-flowing pictures of other folks and their active lives. As a high school senior, she is now more beautiful, more self-confident, quite self-directed, and eager to begin her new life in college.

One day long ago, after I had given her a little book for inspiration, she left a pink letter on my desk.

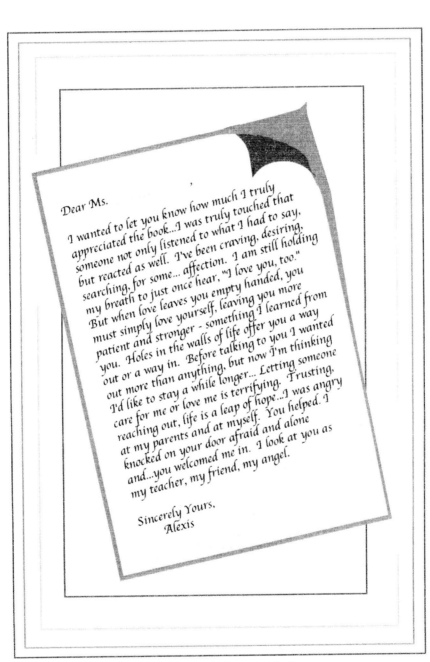

Dear Ms.

I wanted to let you know how much I truly appreciated the book...I was truly touched that someone not only listened to what I had to say, but reacted as well. I've been craving, desiring, searching, for some... affection. I am still holding my breath to just once hear, "I love you, too." But when love leaves you empty handed, you must simply love yourself, leaving you more patient and stronger - something I learned from you. Holes in the walls of life offer you a way out or a way in. Before talking to you I wanted out more than anything, but now I'm thinking I'd like to stay a while longer... Letting someone care for me or love me is terrifying. Trusting, reaching out, life is a leap of hope...I was angry at my parents and at myself. You helped. I knocked on your door afraid and alone and...you welcomed me in. I look at you as my teacher, my friend, my angel.

Sincerely Yours,
Alexis

11.3. Letter *by Anonymous Student*

12.1. Gary's Signs *by Anonymous Photographer*

⑫

THE ULTIMATE VIEW

Throughout my life, there have been many instances when I wanted to know more than humans can know, to reach on earth the understanding of life that awaits us only after death. During the spring and early summer of 1998, I learned the most valuable lessons of all about life and teaching. Sadly, I learned them by seeing my husband's life from the ultimate view.

How Gary Smith came to be a teacher, even he was never sure. He was the first in his family to achieve a bachelor's degree. He was a big brother and in many ways the head of his family. Since he was seven, his father had appeared in his life only five times. Until Gary was forty-five, he believed that being deserted by his father had no effect on him at all.

Gary made average grades in high school, though he was a creative and gifted thinker. His mother was the principal's secretary, and Gary had amusing stories to tell about his encounters with her on his way to the principal's office. He was also an athlete and a fluent communicator.

Gary became a teacher in the days when lower-middle-class people did not consider becoming doctors or lawyers, and athletes chose teaching so that they could coach. Gary became an English teacher and track coach, par excellence. His success, however, was not measurable through standardized tests or state championships, though his teams won three state, seven regional, fifteen district, and fourteen league championships and he was selected District Coach of the Year eighteen times. Gary would always slough off attention paid to his victories and honors. One time he refused to be recognized on local television as the teacher of the week because he was too embarrassed at the messiness of his classroom. He was most pleased, however, when he was chosen to receive the state coaching association's award for sportsmanship and ethics.

For Gary, success was counted one student at a time. He never taught an honors class or even a senior-level class. He made his mark quietly, working with students everyone else avoided, the blue jays. He spent seventeen years teaching a vocational class for ninth-grade potential dropouts who called themselves "Sweathogs" after the 1970s television show *Welcome Back Kotter*. His Sweathogs loved him and worked hard in his classes. One of them was a fat-faced, black-haired fourteen-year-old who called himself "Boogie Bob."

Gary had a remarkable way of making you feel loved even when he was "giving you hell." Therefore, his students learned to function in school society while they were, also, building a sense of self-worth and dignity. On the track, his athletes were treated the same way: They did not get away with cutting corners during practice, they learned the joy of reaching their own potentials, they felt valuable and loved, even the "also-rans." Gary helped his athletes and students deal with myriad personal problems that included physical abuse, sexual abuse, and anorexia. He made invisible students feel important and victorious ones support their slower teammates.

Gary was also a straight talker and had little stomach for school politics. As a result, there were those who disliked him. He wasn't always on time to class, his organizational skills were deficient, and his language was not always "appropriate." Tidy, perfectionist, and emotionally reserved teachers were sometimes offended or at least befuddled by him. But principals and guidance counselors approached him repeatedly to teach their most difficult, sensitive, and emotionally needy young people. Thus, Gary taught on his own terms—according to his values—for thirty-one years.

Christmas at the Smith household in 1997 was irritable. Nothing seemed quite right, almost as if a pall had descended on the family. By

January, the virus Gary thought he had been carrying worsened, and on Saturday morning, January 9, he woke up jaundiced. The next week he had a series of medical tests that each delivered progressively worse news. On January 13, a doctor handed me a piece of paper to take to the lab. It read "Pa. Ca." I knew the abbreviations. Gary had one of the most vicious forms of cancer: pancreatic.

He lived the expected number of months. The operative word is *lived*. He immediately set up his retirement and called in sick for the rest of his life. But he did not stop coaching. He went to practice every day that he was not in the hospital. He attended every weekly meet, the District, and the Regional. He coached his state finalists by phone from his bed at Hospice. Gary *lived* his last five months exactly as he wanted to. He told me once, as he sat on the front porch pondering his death, that he was not afraid. He also told me what he wanted his students to know: "Nothing has really changed. I still get each up each morning and decide how I want to live."

But something had changed. The people whose lives he had touched woke up. Within a few days of his diagnosis, he began getting cards and calls from all over the world. Former students from as many as thirty years ago and as far away as Japan, Europe, and South America were acknowledging the impact he had had on their lives. "Get Well" cards came to the house in piles.

At first he didn't get it. Why were they telling him all these nice things? But gradually he began to accept the great love and respect for him that his students were communicating. He was one of the lucky ones who got to hear the praise while he was still alive.

Gary Smith died at 2:50 PM on June 10, the last day of school. Then, in the depths of great sorrow, our family witnessed indescribable beauty. Students made over thirty bed-sheet signs and hung them along the fence that bordered the high school track at the main entrance into town. The sheets proclaimed love and admiration for their teacher/coach in spiritual and philosophical sayings, such as Flavia's, "Some people come into our lives and quickly leave; others leave footprints on our hearts and we are never the same again" (Weeden and Weeden, 1999, p. 115). The students' words escorted Gary onward and told of the enormous good he had done in this world. Athletes made a make-shift shrine where they lit candles every night, and left long messages to Gary along with their varsity letters and championship medals. The shrine grew for eleven days until a Celebration of Life Ceremony was held for Gary.

It was estimated that nearly eight hundred people attended—students and parents from the 1960s, 1970s, 1980s, and 1990s; coaches from around the state; reporters; friends; colleagues; and family. As a result of the thousands of dollars of gifts received, the Gary Smith Compassionate Teaching Award was established to recognize local teachers for exceptional acts of kindness toward students. Articles about Gary's character and contribution to young people's lives appeared in all the local newspapers. On the cover of one was a picture of a dark-haired, round-faced, thirty-eight-year-old man standing solemnly by Gary's shrine. It was Boogie Bob from the Sweathog class of 1976.

There are many possible responses to the story of Gary's life and death. This is mine. As Gary's wife, and later his widow, I learned that a teacher's reach extends around the world. Though our work is local and our efforts seem small, the effects of our teaching spread through our students wherever they stop to live. Our reach extends, as well, into unseen decades, because our influence affects our students' future families and future work.

The message I derived from Gary's passing is this: How we treat our students matters greatly! Every act of kindness, moment of understanding, or gift of wisdom expands. When we touch one life, our touch multiplies exponentially.

So do the thoughtless and hurtful ways we respond to our students. When we teach achievement without teaching integrity, cheaters develop. When we stress competition without compassion, selfishness grows. When we demand obedience without also showing students how to follow their own lead, creativity dies. When we punish without ferreting out root causes of behavior, we increase suffering and failure. When we focus on what young people do wrong instead of celebrating with awe the value of each person who enters our classrooms, we darken the world.

The reaction in Gary's community to his death shows the magnitude of a teacher's impact. Every day we educators change the world, one child a time, hundreds or thousands of children per teacher; think of the millions of encounters with young people we have during our careers.

As letters sent to me at the time of Gary's death document, teaching compassionately can break prejudices, stimulate growth, change characters, and heal hearts. It counteracts entropy.

Let us take care to respond to each of our students in ways that enlighten and nurture. Let us send every child out into the world with self-worth, creativity, hope, and love. As Gary would ask us to do, let us wake up each morning and decide how we want to live and how we want teach.

REFERENCES

Amabile, T. (1983). Motivation to create. In S. G. Isaksen (Ed.), *Frontiers of Creativity Research*. Buffalo, NY: Bearly Limited.

American Association of University Women. www.aauw.org.

American Psychiatric Association. (2000). Diagnostic and statistical manual of mental disorders (4th ed.). Washington, DC: American Psychiatric Association.

American Psychological Association. (2004). www.apa.org/pubinfo/anger.html.

Banks, J. (1994). *An introduction to multi-cultural education*. Boston: Allyn & Bacon.

Benson, P., Williams, D., and Johnson, A. (1987). *The quicksilver years: The hopes and fears of early adolescence*. San Francisco: Harper & Row.

Berger, J. (1977) *Ways of Seeing*. New York: Penguin.

Bloom, B. S. (1956). *Taxonomy of educational objectives*. New York: David McKay Company.

———. (Ed.). (1985). *Developing talent in young people*. New York: Ballentine Books.

Bode, C. (Ed.). (1975). *The portable Thoreau*. New York: Penguin Books.

Brendtro, L., Brokenleg, M., and Bockern, S. (1998). *Reclaiming youth at risk: Our hope for the future*. Bloomington, IN: National Educational Service.

Briggs-Myers, I. (1990). *Gifts differing*. Palo Alto, CA: Consulting Psychologists Press, Inc.

Center for Media Literacy. (2004). www.medialit.org.

The Color Purple [film]. (1985). (S. Spielberg, Dir.) Warner Studios.

Conroy, P. (2002). *My losing season*. New York: Doubleday.

Csikszentmihalyi, M., Rathunde, K., and Whalen, S. (1993). *Talented teenagers*. Cambridge: Cambridge University Press.

Erikson, E. H. (1950). *Childhood and society*. New York: Norton.

Gilligan, C. (1982). *In a different voice*. Cambridge: Harvard University Press.

Glasser, W. (1969). *Schools without failure*. New York: Harper and Row.

———. (1992). *The quality school*. New York: Harper Perennial.

Hallowell, E. M., and Ratey, J. (1994). *Driven to distraction*. New York: Simon & Schuster.

Herman, J. (1997). *Trauma and recovery*. New York: Basic Books.

Hoffman, D., and Levak, B. A. (2003). Personalizing schools. *Educational Leadership*, 30–43.

Interfaith Center for Peace. peace-center.org.

Kirby, P. (1979). *Cognitive style, learning style, and transfer skill acquisition*. Columbus, OH: Ohio State University, National Center for Research in Vocational Education.

Kohn, A. (1993). *Punished by rewards*. New York: Houghton Mifflin.

Languis, M. L., Naour, P., Buffer, J. J., and Martin, D. J. (1986). *Cognitive science and educational practice*. Columbus, OH: Educational Research and Information Center, Ohio State University.

Lawrence, G. (1982). *People types and tiger stripes*. Gainesville, FL: Association for Psychological Type.

Levine, M. (2002). *A mind at a time*. New York: Simon and Schuster.

Martindale, C., and Armstrong, J. (1974). The relationship of creativity to cortical activation and its operant control. *The Journal of Genetic Psychology, 124*, 311–320.

Maslow, A. (1968). *Toward a psychology of being* (2nd ed.). New York: Van Nostrand Reinhold.

May, R. (1969). *Love and will*. New York: Delta.

———. (1975). *The courage to create*. New York: W. W. Norton & Co., Inc.

Menninger, K. (1982). The church's responsibility for the homeless. In R. Gillogly (Ed.), *Sacred shelters*. Topeka, KS: The Villages.

Mind over media [video]. (2001). Santa Monica, CA: Center for Media Literacy.

Newman, B., and Newman, P. (1978). *Infancy and childhood*. New York: Wiley and Sons.

Oremus, E. (2004, January). *Improving self management skills of ADHD children: What should we be doing differently?* Presented at Marburn Academy Community Parent Seminar, Columbus, Ohio.

Peck, S. (1978). *The road less traveled*. New York: Simon & Schuster.

Piaget, J. (1975). The development of thought: Equilibrium of cognitive structures (A. Rosin, Trans.). New York: Viking.

Piaget, J., and Inhelder, I. (1969). *The psychology of the child.* (H. Weaver, Trans.). New York: Basic Books. (Original work published 1966.)

Prelude to a Kiss [film]. (1992). (N. Rene, Dir.) Twentieth Century Fox.

Restak, R. (1984). The brain. New York: Bantam.

Skinner, B. F. (1974). *About behaviorism.* New York: Vintage.

Spitzmueller, M., and James, K. (2002). *This is not a book.* Baltimore: America House.

Springer, S., and Deutsch, G. (1981). *Left brain, right brain.* San Francisco: W.H. Freeman & Co.

Teaching Tolerance. www.tolerance.org/teach.

Webster's third unabridged dictionary. (1986). Chicago: Encyclopedia Britannica, Inc.

Weeden, F., and Weeden, L. (1999). *Forever.* San Rafael, CA: Cedco Publishing Co.

White, R. (1959). Motivation reconsidered: The concept of competence. *Psychological Review, 66,* 297–333.

Wilson, L. (1997). *Ceramics: Shape and surface.* L. Wilson.

INDEX

abuse, 7, 12, 17, 22–23, 40, 64, 69, 77, 95, 116

absence, 20, 28

aggression, 17, 19, 22–24, 41–43, 48, 56, 84, 88, 94

Amabile, Teresa, 66

anger management, 16, 28

apathy, 2, 20, 23–25, 27, 29, 88, 91, 101

Attention Deficit Disorder, 79, 81

attitude problems, 7, 23, 26, 34

authority, authoritarian, 59–62, 88, 96

behavior:
  attention-seeking, 36, 76–78, 91
  root/underlying causes, xii, 7, 8, 19, 22–23, 25, 28, 70, 78, 94–96, 101, 104, 118

behavior modification. *See* reward and punishment

behaviorism. *See* reward and punishment

blaming, 23–24, 56, 69, 84, 105

bullying, 19, 22, 48

care, caring, 20, 22, 32–37, 40–41, 48, 77, 95–96, 100–1, 110

carelessness, 75–76, 79

character, 12, 24, 29 96–97, 101, 119

Circle of Courage, 34

closure, 5–7, 73

cognitive styles. *See* learning styles

compassion, xiii, 7, 62, 67, 96–9, 104, 110–11, 115, 118–19
  Ten Objectives for Effective Compassionate Teaching, 103–05

competition, 62–65, 114, 118

conflict resolution, 13, 15–17, 28, 40

consequences, natural, real, 28, 44, 93–94. *See also* reward and punishment

coping mechanisms, 7, 16, 29

courage, xiii, 40, 87, 90–93, 96–101

creativity, creative growth, 1– 3, 38–39, 47, 61–62, 69, 71–72, 79, 87–88, 93, 98–100, 104, 115, 118–19
creative thinking, 45, 94
highly creative people, 73–75

déjà vu, 6–7
differentiated teaching, 17, 29, 30–31, 49, 77, 98–100. *See also* teaching methods
dignity, 28, 62,79, 84, 88, 91, 92, 116
discipline, 11, 94, 96
self, 29, 47–8
Seven-Step Plan for Positive Discipline, 93
disequilibrium, 47–48
dissociation, 21
dropping out of school, 20, 83
dysgraphia, 30, 76, 78–79

eating disorders, 40, 42, 48, 69, 111–13, 116
empowerment, xii, 11, 29, 41–49, 56, 60, 62, 65, 88, 103–4
entropy, 1–3, 11, 17, 25, 29, 38, 41, 56, 62, 65, 88, 100, 103, 119
etiquette, 16, 61,

failure, 2, 7, 20–22, 24, 26, 28–29, 63, 66, 81–82, 84, 95, 118

growth, 2, 3, 12–13, 24, 27–29, 38, 47, 56, 61–62, 66, 68, 88, 90, 94, 98, 101, 119. *See also* creativity

irresponsibility, 72–75. *See also* responsibility

knowledge, xii, 11–17, 39, 44, 56, 61
Kohn, Alfie, 66

labels, labeling, 5–7, 59, 69–79
laziness, 7, 25, 70–72, 79
learning:
disabilities, 76, 78–81
styles 13, 15–17, 26, 27, 29–31, 40, 45, 49, 61, 70, 73, 75–6, 78–79
life skills, 13–15, 17, 45
limits, 32, 41, 43–45, 88, 96. *See also* rules
listening, 7, 13–15, 17, 28, 39, 40, 53, 78, 101, 104, 110
love, xii–xiii, 7, 32–41, 47–49, 52–53, 56, 82, 100, 103, 110, 112, 116–117, 119

Maslow, Abraham, xii, 11, 34
May, Rollo, 9, 99–100
media literacy, 13, 15
mediation. *See* conflict resolution
mental health, 7, 8, 15–17, 21–27, 29, 84–5
mood disorders, 17, 25–27, 40, 48, 109. *See also* mental health
motivation, 7, 25, 27, 29, 31, 38, 65
competence, 29, 30–31, 42, 82, 105
extrinsic, 66–7
intrinsic, 66–68, 83, 90
See also behavior, underlying causes

Native American practices. *See* Circle of Courage
nurturing, 20, 79, 87, 90–1, 93–94, 96, 119

Oremus, Earl, 20, 41, 43, 81
organization, 73–75, 78–9, 88–9, 116

passive-aggression, 20, 21, 56
personal records (P.R.s), 63–65, 68

Piaget, Jean, xii, 13, 47
perfectionism, 42, 116
personality types, 17, 26
political arena, activism, xiii, 72, 104
power struggles, 27, 92
prejudice, 13, 15–17
problem solving, 12, 14,16, 27–28, 31, 69–93, 95–96, 100
problem students, 52–53, 68–69
prejudice. *See* racism
psychology, developmental, 7, 13–15, 17, 40, 47, 84

racism, 13, 15–17
rebellion, 7, 43, 48–49, 63
relationship, xii–xiii, 8, 12–13, 35, 60–62, 68, 87, 106
building, 95–96, 100
respect, 28, 59, 62, 91, 94, 96, 117
reward and punishment, 2, 12–14, 24–29, 56, 62, 72, 75, 81–85, 87, 90–91, 96, 104, 118. *See also* extrinsic motivation
rules, 13–14, 88, 90–1, 106

self:
artificial, 17, 60,
creative, 19, 42, 44, 47

essential, inner, 19, 20, 32, 51, 111
self-esteem, worth, 7, 24, 27–29, 60, 64, 66, 69, 71, 75, 79, 82, 91, 110, 116, 119
self-protection, 11, 17–31, 71, 91, 103–4
cocoons, 31, 40, 51, 53
sexism. *See* prejudice
Smith, Gary, 27, 35, 45, 65–66,109–111, 114–120
society, 64, 80, 94
social caste system, 83–85
substance abuse, 7, 17, 40, 42–3, 48, 53, 69
success, 29, 31, 41, 45, 51, 53, 65–67, 71–72, 84

tardiness, 28, 72–74
time-management, 73–75
teaching methods, 45–46, 67, 71

varying. *See* differentiated teaching
time-outs, 18, 92
truths worth laboring for, xii, 105

vision, 4–9, 106
as world view, 6

ABOUT THE AUTHOR

Dr. Nicole M. Gnezda has been an educator and advocate for student-centered teaching since 1973. Her experience includes pre-kindergarten, elementary, middle school, high school, and university-level teaching. She has taught in several school districts in the Columbus, Ohio area.

Currently, she teaches Visual Art at Worthington Kilbourne High School, a nationally recognized Blue Ribbon School in the Worthington (Ohio) City School District. During her career, she started Creative Mondays, a student group that uses the arts to address life issues. She is also the founder and administrator of the Gary Smith Compassionate Teaching Award, presented annually to an exemplary staff member of the Worthington Schools.

Her own education includes a bachelor of fine arts degree from Ohio Wesleyan University, a master of arts and doctorate from The Ohio State University. The focuses of her Ph.D. studies were creativity and learning. In addition to her teaching and writing, Dr. Gnezda loves to make art, write poetry, cook, garden, and be in the natural world. She is married and the mother of three awesome children.